# FILL MY STOCKING

# Fill my Stocking

Compiled,
partially written and
totally illustrated by Alan Titchmarsh

**BBC**
BOOKS

*For Bob and Steve*
(serves them right)

Published by BBC Books, BBC Worldwide Limited,
80 Wood Lane, London W12 0TT

First published 2005

Reprinted 2005

ISBN 0 563 48862 X

Commissioning editor: Nicky Ross
Project editors: Helena Caldon and Sarah Reece
Designer: Linda Blakemore
Copy editor: Tessa Clark
Production controller: Kenneth McKay

Set in Simoncini Garamond
Printed and bound in Great Britain by Butler and Tanner Ltd

# Contents

# Introduction

I sat down with my oldest friend last Christmas and sipped a glass of whisky. We've known each other for around 30 years now. He's a solicitor. We were seated on either side of a log fire, and as he gazed into the flickering flames he looked a bit fed up. I asked him what was the matter. 'I'm worried,' he admitted.

'About what?' I asked.

'About not being funny any more. I don't want to become too serious while I'm growing older. I mean, I want to keep being silly.'

I looked at him, crouched over his glass of single malt, and raised an eyebrow.

'I mean,' he said, 'I think it's important that I'm stupid some of the time.'

I told him, quite firmly, that as far as I was concerned he was one of the most stupid people I knew, and he smiled a broad smile, happy that so far at least he had escaped being completely grown up.

It was Beatrix Potter who said that to enjoy life to the full it was important to keep a bit of the child in you, and at Christmas it strikes me as being especially important. I feel sorry for those people for whom Christmas is just an excuse to be grumpy about the descending relations, ill-tempered about the price of cards and bilious about the commercialization of it all. Yes, there are those for whom Christmas can be a sad time – due to circumstances beyond their own control – but I am determined, along with my friend, that Christmas, even more than any other time of the year, is a season for being stupid or, perhaps more accurately, childlike.

But then I've always been a fan of the festive season. A lot of the credit for this must go to my dad. When I was five or six years old I could never work out why the cellar of our tiny Yorkshire terrace house was always declared out of bounds from October to Christmas. Perhaps it was just full of coal to keep us warm in winter. But every evening, it seemed, my father was down there banging away at something with his hammer. The smell of new paint would waft upwards through the cellar door, and in my childish innocence it never occurred to me to tiptoe down the stairs and see what he was up to.

8

I accepted without demur that he must be making a new piece of furniture for my mother, or repairing an old chair (Mum was forever swapping our dining chairs at the saleroom at the bottom of our street – everything from Arts and Crafts to Ercol graced our tiny living room), and Dad was a dab hand at DIY.

Even on Christmas morning, when a castellated fort with moat, drawbridge and soldiers, or a red-and-yellow painted zoo, complete with animals, appeared at the bottom of my bed, I made no connection with the fact that the cellar was once again opened up to all comers, and that there was nothing to be seen down there except a slithering heap of nutty slack, an acrid-smelling jam jar full of paintbrushes and a neat pile of sawdust.

'Has he been yet?' was the plaintive cry from my sister and myself on Christmas morning at anything from five o'clock onwards. 'No; go back to sleep,' muttered my exhausted, woodworking dad from under the covers of the parental double bed.

I remember on one Christmas morning being bitterly disappointed at the relatively empty pillowcase on the

bottom of my eiderdown, only to discover a train-set on a massive board laid out in front of the sitting-room fire when I got downstairs. 'Father Christmas had a job getting it upstairs,' explained my father, suppressing a smile. His smile gave way to a puzzled expression later that morning when, having run the train around the track a few times and parked it in the siding, I went on to spend the rest of the day building a cut-out theatre from a one-and-sixpenny book that I'd found in the pillow-case. But I still loved my train, and over the weeks that followed I painted roadways on the board, and then green fields, and I made trees from small bits of green-painted loofah.

In the run-up to Christmas I'd have my own job to do. Nothing to do with Christmas shopping or baking – other than the obligatory stirring of the Christmas cake some weeks before. Mum never put any sixpences or silver threepenny bits into it as some mums did. She said she was worried about my Auntie Alice breaking a tooth on one of them, and as Auntie Alice's health was suspect at the best of times, I don't think my mother wanted to give her another excuse to take to her bed.

No; my own job in the run-up to Christmas was carol singing. None of your ad hoc three friends and half a caterwauled verse of 'Good King Wenceslas' for me. I went up the better end of town along with the other boys from the church choir. In the 1950s, before we were all so charity conscious, we were allowed to sing door to door and to split the takings between ourselves. We sang on just two nights – Christmas Eve and the night before – and our very last port of call on Christmas Eve was an enormous house at the top of Grove Road – Ilkley's smartest residential street. We would be invited in from the chilly gloom, grouped around the drawing-room grand piano played by the church organist, and treated, after our comprehensive rendition from the carol sheet, to orange squash and biscuits.

The house itself had a spectacular galleried staircase and, on being told that I was keen on painting, the lady of the house took me on a tour of the works of art that hung on the walls of the enormous hall. There were country landscapes and sea scenes, and one particular picture of a youth, casually leaning on a tree, sticks in my mind. 'This is my son,' said Mrs B. 'I'm not too sure about the likeness but I said I would always know it was my son because of his hands.' I remember feeling rather sad that the painter had not lived up to expectations in the face department.

Christmas Day and Boxing Day were a mix and match affair of visits to the houses of relations and the returning of hospitality at our house in Nelson Road. Uncle Bert and Auntie Edie would always give a good children's and grown-ups' party in the rooms above their grocer's shop – always augmented with the aroma of freshly ground coffee – and Boxing Day tea was usually with grandma and Auntie Alice in their miniature front room in Dean Street – the square table taking up almost all the available space, and its rough, green-baize cover

studded with plates of boiled ham and pickled onions, buttered slices of white bread, stand pie, mince pies and Christmas cake of dubious vintage.

If I close my eyes, I can relive those early Christmases and feel those same feelings of excited anticipation. My own children are 25 and 23 now, but I hope they, too, have memories of their own childhood Christmases that will warm them in future winter weather.

As a family nowadays, we have quiet Christmases together, but for the last 19 years, on the Sunday before Christmas, we've invited friends to a homespun Christmas entertainment in a large room attached to the old house, or nowadays in the barn next door to the new one. The title of the evening's offering gives little away – 'Christmas Spice' or 'Festive Frolics' – but everyone who comes and stuffs themselves with warm mince pies and a glass or two of wine, knows that as well as being given a chance to sing themselves hoarse with carols, they'll also be able to laugh at an extremely silly entertainment purveyed for their delectation by the Titchmice and their friends. There might be a pocket-sized panto or a groan-worthy monologue, an over-the-top melodrama or a musical interlude. But whatever the nature of the entertainment, the sight of several rows of expectant faces, lit by the glow of footlights and candles, has become, for me, the essence of Christmas present. This family entertainment is now a Christmas tradition every bit as fixed in the calendar as Boxing Day tea at grandma's and the filling of stockings and pillowcases.

As far as my friend is concerned, there is little cause for concern. He will continue in the tradition he has long since upheld, to put aside the day job during the festive season and play the fool, and the audience will laugh and smile indulgently – as they have done for the last 19 years. There is, as far as I can see, not the remotest chance of him ever growing up. With any luck, the rest of us will also manage to give Peter Pan a good run for his money.

What follows is a stockingful of these Christmas bits and pieces, collected and written over the years to cheer up our friends at the start of the festive season; to make them smile, to prick their eyes with a tear, but, above all, to make Christmas a bit special. With any luck, they'll do the same for you.

Happy Christmas!

# A YORKSHIRE CHRISTMAS

I moved 'down south' when I was 19 and, as yet, I've not moved back. 'If Yorkshire is such a wonderful place,' people ask me, 'why do you live down here?' My answer is that I am doing missionary work.

But then, as a member of the All England Lawn Tennis Club remarked when she introduced me prior to my after-dinner speech: 'Yorkshire men who move down south are like haemorrhoids. If they come down and go back up they are no bother. But if they come down and stay down they are a pain in the arse.'

Ever conscious of my migration to warmer climes, my late mother used to love it when Alison, the kids and I all piled back home at Christmas, but her nervousness at my assumed southern ways became more clearly pronounced, until, one Christmas, she gave me the list on the page opposite to fill in.

Newcomers to Yorkshire might like to look at it and test their understanding of the language spoken by some of the local people.

Time allowed: 20 minutes

1 Initot?
2 Giusit.
3 Summatsupeer.
4 Gerritetten.
5 Supwidee?
6 Smarrerweeim?
7 Iampgorrit.
8 Aster gorrit withy?
9 Purremineer.
10 Ayampt eared nowt.
11 Thalafter gerra newun.
12 Eesezitintis burra-
   berritis.
13 Lerrus gerrus anzwesht.
14 Sumenemz gorragerroff.
15 We've gorra gerrus
   imbux.
16 Thamun gerrit learnt.
17 Shut thigob.
18 Aberritinters.
19 Putwuddintoil.
20 Nardendee,
   wotdardoin?
21 Asta sinnim ont telly?
22 Corferus arpastate
   intmornin.
23 It dunt marrer.
24 Lerrus gurrat pixchers.
25 Astagorratanner?
26 Eenose nowt abartit.
27 Eez gunna gerra lorra
   lolly forrit.
28 Lerram gerrintbus.
29 Eddursnt purrised
   undert watter.

30 Eeseziantaddit.
31 Oowereewe; wurree
   weezsen?
32 Ateldim burree
   wuntlissen.
33 Astle clowte thee iftha
   dunt gioer.
34 Lerrim purrizaton.
35 Tintintin.
36 Gerarry tergithi
   andweeit.
37 Eez gorriz atoam.
38 Thawanster wesh thi
   erroils aht.
39 Thakkan iftha wonts.
40 Eez nobbutta babbi.
41 Tantad nowt dunnatit
   as I nose on.
42 Middads gorrajag.
43 Cantha kumtoowerowse
   tunneet?
44 Weers gaffar?
45 Purrersaspeshlinjack.
46 Itsdarnintcoiloil.
47 Shintin.
48 Thaluckswell;
   estabinill?
49 Wysta mytherin?
50 Tekme buitsoff less;
   evedi gruiller.

*Answers overleaf*

1 Warm, isn't it?
2 Please hand me that object.
3 I detect that all is not well.
4 I suggest you clear your plate.
5 What is the matter?
6 Does he have a problem?
7 The object you seek is not in my possession.
8 Are you in possession of it?
9 Place them in my receptacle.
10 It's news to me.
11 This could be expensive.
12 Although he is denying ownership, I am not sure that I believe him.
13 Where is the bathroom?
14 In order for us to board the bus, several passengers will have to alight first.
15 Good morning, Vicar.
16 Please try to memorize the information.
17 Be quiet.
18 I am suspicious of her rightful ownership.
19 Shut the door.
20 Good morning! How are you?
21 Is he a celebrity?
22 I'll be ready at 0800 hours.
23 It dunt marrer.
24 Would you care to accompany me to the cinema?
25 Do you have two-and-a-half new pence?
26 He is ignorant.
27 Nice little earner.
28 Please allow the ladies on first.
29 He is afraid of drowning.
30 A likely story.
31 Was he alone?
32 Serves him right.
33 If you don't refrain from that activity, I shall be forced to assault you physically.
34 Encourage him to wear headgear.
35 It in't in't tin.
36 Harold will help you.
37 Alas, he left it behind.
38 Are you deaf?
39 Suit yourself.
40 a) He's far too young, or
   b) You'll be arrested.
41 It is in its original condition.
42 My father is John Prescott.

43 Fancy a coffee?
44 Is the boss about?
45 Might I have a larger piece of cod with my chips?
46 I left it in the cellar.
47 My mother/wife/sister/girlfriend/granny is out.
48 You look much better than you did.
49 What's up?
50 Would you mind removing my footwear, darling? I've had a bit of a day.

How did you do?

10 correct answers – on your way to being a settler

40 correct answers – presumably you're from Sheffield

All correct – time you brushed up on your Queen's English

# Christmas is Coming

*Anticipation is the key to Christmas – the ultimate in travelling hopefully. If for some reason the day itself comes as an anticlimax, then at least the run-up can be full of hope and pleasure. The pieces I write for Christmas are always written for the voice – to be read out loud. I am embarrassed at the naivety of some of them on the page. But if they are read well, they need not sound mawkish, and Christmas is a time for pureness of sentiment.*

# LIKE IT WAS
*Alan Titchmarsh*

'Twas the night before Christmas
Not too long ago
When the streets of the town
Were all covered in snow.

No rain filled the gutters
No wind shook the tree
The trains were on time
And the traffic ran free.

But still, though we're warmed
By those global effects
And programmes on telly
Are all about sex,

We've managed to cling to
The hopes and the joys
That we had when we were
Little girls, little boys.

When we used 'old money'
And apples would store well
And Blair was the real name
Of writer George Orwell.

When prime ministers' wives
Lived at Chartwell in Kent
Instead of in Bristol
With two flats to rent.

When my dad gave my mum
A new perfume called 'Heaven'
And Westlife was something
You found down in Devon.

There were nuts and satsumas
Roast goose and high teas
Instead of Nigella
Cellphones and CDs.

But in spite of the changes
The fastness of life,
Through it all shines the tale
Of a man and his wife.

They journeyed at night
Through darkness and danger
To give birth to a son
In a dusty old manger.

*This is the earliest Christmas poem I can remember. We would stand on Yorkshire doorsteps chanting this to our grannies, aunts and uncles. They never gave us anything.*

## CHRISTMAS IS COMING
*Anon*

Christmas is coming,
　The goose is getting fat,
Please put a penny
　In the old man's hat.
If you haven't got a penny,
　A ha'penny will do;
If you haven't got a ha'penny,
　Then God bless you!

## CHRISTMAS
*John Betjeman*

The bells of waiting Advent ring,
     The Tortoise stove is lit again
And lamp-oil light across the night
     Has caught the streets of winter rain
In many a stained-glass window sheen
From Crimson Lake to Hooker's Green.

The holly in the windy hedge
     And round the Manor House the yew
Will soon be stripped to deck the ledge,
     The altar, font and arch and pew,
So that the villagers can say
'The church looks nice' on Christmas Day.

Provincial public houses blaze
     And Corporation tramcars clang,
On lighted tenements I gaze

Where paper decorations hang,
And bunting in the red Town Hall
Says 'Merry Christmas to you all'.

And London shops on Christmas Eve
    Are strung with silver bells and flowers
As hurrying clerks the City leave
    To pigeon-haunted classic towers,
And marbled clouds go scudding by
The many-steepled London sky.

And girls in slacks remember Dad,
    And oafish louts remember Mum,
And sleepless children's hearts are glad,
    And Christmas-morning bells say 'Come!'
Even to shining ones who dwell
Safe in the Dorchester Hotel.

And is it true? And is it true,
    This most tremendous tale of all,
Seen in a stained-glass window's hue,
    A Baby in an ox's stall?
The Maker of the stars and sea
Become a Child on earth for me?

And is it true? For if it is,
    No loving fingers tying strings
Around those tissued fripperies,
    The sweet and silly Christmas things,

Bath salts and inexpensive scent
And hideous tie so kindly meant,

No love that in a family dwells,
   No carolling in frosty air,
Nor all the steeple-shaking bells
   Can with this single Truth compare –
That God was Man in Palestine
And lives today in Bread and Wine.

## JINGLE BELLS
*James Pierpont*

Dashing through the snow,
In a one-horse open sleigh;
O'er the fields we go,
Laughing all the way;
Bells on bob-tail ring,
Making spirits bright;
Oh what fun to ride and sing
A sleighing song tonight.

Jingle bells, jingle bells,
Jingle all the way;
Oh! What joy it is to ride
In a one-horse open sleigh.
Jingle bells, jingle bells,
Jingle all the way;
Oh! What joy it is to ride
In a one-horse open sleigh.

*The right sort of weather can turn a good Christmas into a great Christmas. We need snow, or at the very least, crisp and frosty mornings where breath comes out in clouds and frosted patterns creep over the window pane. Edward Thomas died in the First World War. He was a country poet from my part of Hampshire, so his words always seem especially appropriate. Shakespeare conjures up images of the unwashed and unlovely 'greasy Joan' as she stirs her bubbling cauldron, and John Clare remains the best of all the country poets. Clive Sansom sums up the beauty of a single snowflake perfectly.*

SNOW
*Edward Thomas*

In the gloom of whiteness,
In the great silence of snow,
    A child was sighing
    And bitterly saying: 'Oh,
They have killed a white bird up there on her nest,
The down is fluttering from her breast.'
And still it fell through that dusky brightness
On the child crying for the bird of the snow.

# From LOVE'S LABOUR'S LOST
*William Shakespeare*

When icicles hang by the wall,
And Dick the shepherd blows his nail,
And Tom bears logs into the hall,
    And milk comes frozen home in pail.
When blood is nipped and ways be foul,
Then nightly sings the staring owl,
               Tu-who;
Tu-whit, tu-who: a merry note,
While greasy Joan doth keel the pot.

When all aloud the wind doth blow,
    And coughing drowns the parson's saw,
And birds sit brooding in the snow,
    And Marian's nose looks red and raw,
When roasted crabs hiss in the bowl,
Then nightly sings the staring owl,
               Tu-who;
Tu-whit, tu-who: a merry note
While greasy Joan doth keel the pot.

# DECEMBER
## From THE SHEPHERD'S CALENDAR
*John Clare*

While snows the window-panes bedim,
    The fire curls up a sunny charm,
Where, creaming o'er the pitcher's rim,
    The flowering ale is set to warm.
Mirth, full of joy as summer bees,
    Sits there, its pleasures to impart,
And children, 'tween their parents' knees,
    Sing scraps of carols o'er by heart.

And some, to view the winter weathers,
    Climb up the window-seat with glee,
Likening the snow to falling feathers,
    In Fancy's infant ecstasy;
Laughing, with superstitious love,
    O'er visions wild that youth supplies,
Of people pulling geese above,
    And keeping Christmas in the skies.

As though the homestead trees were dressed,
    In lieu of snow, with dancing leaves;
As though the sun-dried martin's nest,
    Instead of icicles, hung the eaves,
The children hail the happy day,
    As if the snow were April's grass;
And pleased, as 'neath the warmth of May,
    Sport o'er the water froze to glass.

# SNOWFLAKES
*Clive Sansom*

And did you know
That every flake of snow
That forms so high
In the grey winter sky,
And falls so far
Is a bright six-pointed star?
Each crystal grows
A flower as perfect as a rose.
Lace could never make
The patterns of a flake.
No brooch
Of figured silver could approach
Its delicate craftsmanship. And think:
Each pattern is distinct.
Of all the snowflakes floating there –
The million million in the air –
None is the same. Each star
Is newly forged, as faces are,
Shaped to its own design
Like yours and mine.
And yet … each one
Melts when its flight is done;
Holds frozen loveliness
A moment, even less;
Suspends itself in time –
And passes like a rhyme.

## AN ATROCIOUS INSTITUTION
*George Bernard Shaw*

*The World*, 20 DECEMBER 1893

Like all intelligent people, I greatly dislike Christmas. It revolts me to see a whole nation refrain from music for weeks together in order that every man may rifle his neighbour's pockets under cover of a ghastly general pretence of festivity. It is really an atrocious institution, this Christmas. We must be gluttonous because it is Christmas. We must be drunken because it is Christmas. We must be insincerely generous; we must buy things that nobody wants, and give them to people we don't like; we must go to absurd entertainments that make even our little children satirical; we must writhe under venal officiousness from legions of freebooters, all because it is Christmas – that is, because the mass of the population, including the all-powerful middle-class tradesman, depends on a week of licence and brigandage, waste and intemperance, to clear off its outstanding liabilities at the end of the year. As for me, I shall fly from it all tomorrow or the next day to some remote spot miles from a shop, where nothing worse can befall me than a serenade from a few peasants, or some equally harmless survival of medieval mummery, shyly proffered, not advertised, moderate in its expectations, and soon over. In town there is, for the moment, nothing for me or any honest man to do.


## MISSILES THROUGH THE POST
*Cassandra*

During the next three days about 350 million Christmas cards will be fired in the British Isles … The whole practice is such a thundering nuisance that it is high time that some practical advantage, such as causing unhappiness, was extracted out of the wretched business. I think I can point the way.

The first – and one of the most essential things to decide – is when to shoot. Timing is of critical importance. A premature Christmas card is not only ineffective but can be downright humiliating to the sender. It reveals one's position, discloses the size and weight of the ammunition and often provokes a devastating counter-attack …

The next thing to understand is the value of size in Christmas cards. Important people – and people who think they are important – send big and important-looking Christmas cards. This makes the recipient feel small – which is precisely what was intended. Expensive

Christmas cards can be deadly, too, for they are usually fired by expensive people to make their victims feel cheap. This is often quite costly but well worth it.

The very small Christmas card can be pretty insulting, too. Don't underestimate its destructive value. It shows what you think of the addressee – practically nothing. It is a mistake to make them too small as they then become rather cute and are liable to give pleasure. Avoid this dangerous mistake. A really contemptuous size is about three and a half inches by two and a half inches. They are a bit difficult to obtain in the shops just now but are well worth the suffering they cause.

*Most children's focus at Christmas is on what they are likely to find at the bottom of their bed. For Master Noël Coward there were other things to occupy his mind …*

## THE BOY ACTOR
*Noël Coward*

I can remember. I can remember.
The months of November and December
    Were filled for me with peculiar joys
So different from those of other boys
    For other boys would be counting the days
Until end of term and holiday times
    But I was acting in Christmas plays

While they were taken to pantomimes.
   I didn't envy their Eton suits,
Their children's dances and Christmas trees.
   My life had wonderful substitutes
For such conventional treats as these.
   I didn't envy their country larks,
Their organized games in panelled halls:
   While they made snow-men in stately parks
I was counting the curtain calls.

I remember the auditions, the nerve-racking auditions:
Darkened auditorium and empty, dusty stage,
Little girls in ballet dresses practising 'positions'
Gentlemen with pince-nez asking you your age.
Hopefulness and nervousness struggling within you,
Dreading that familiar phrase, 'Thank you dear, no more.'
Straining every muscle, every tendon, every sinew
To do your dance much better than you'd ever done before.
Think of your performance. Never mind the others,
Never mind the pianist, talent must prevail.
Never mind the baleful eyes of other children's mothers
Glaring from the corners and willing you to fail.

I can remember. I can remember.
The months of November and December
    Were more significant to me
Than other months could ever be
    For they were the months of high romance
When destiny waited on tip-toe,
    When every boy actor stood a chance
Of getting into a Christmas show,
    Not for me the dubious heaven
Of being some prefect's protégé!
    Not for me the Second Eleven.
For me, two performances a day!

Ah those first rehearsals! Only very few lines:
Rushing home to mother, learning them by heart,
'Enter Left through window' – Dots to mark the cue lines:
'Exit with the others' – Still it *was* a part.
Opening performance; legs a bit unsteady,
Dedicated tension, shivers down my spine,
Powder, grease and eye-black, sticks of make-up ready
Leichner number three and number five and number nine.
World of strange enchantment, magic for a small boy
Dreaming of the future, reaching for the crown,
Rigid in the dressing room, listening for the call-boy
'Overture Beginners – Everybody Down!'

I can remember. I can remember.
The months of November and December,
    Although climatically cold and damp,

Meant more to me than Aladdin's lamp.
  I see myself, having got a job,
Walking on wings along the Strand,
  Uncertain whether to laugh or sob
And clutching tightly my mother's hand,
  I never cared who scored the goal
Or which side won the silver cup,
  I never learned to bat or bowl
But I heard the curtain going up.


*There are times when Christmas cannot be celebrated wholeheartedly. Mollie Panter-Downes, the New Yorker's London correspondent, describes one such during the Second World War.*


## CHRISTMAS IN WARTIME
*Mollie Panter-Downes*


The Christmas shops have showed little shortage of the traditional delicacies, except turkeys, which are both scarce and expensive. The big stores came out valiantly with holly-and-cellophane-garlanded signs proclaiming that 'There'll always be a Christmas', and did a rattling good trade in spite of the publicity campaign suggesting that a couple of National Savings Certificates in the toe of the stocking was all that any good citizen could need. Parents have taken advantage of the lull in the Blitz to smuggle children up from the country for a brisk scurry through the toy bazaars, thereby brightening the lives of all the Santas, who had been drooping in their red flannelette and false whiskers among the childless acres of dolls and electric trains.

However unseasonably men may be behaving at this festival of peace on earth and mercy mild, the heavens are contributing a seasonable note. British astronomers are excited over what they call the triple conjunction of Jupiter and Saturn – a spectacle which was last seen in England when Charles II was on the throne and is recorded as one of the strange happenings preceding the birth of Christ. Londoners tacking up the holly in their Anderson shelters are hoping that this will be the only unusual display in the heavens when once more they celebrate that birth on the night of December 25th, 1940.

# Aladdin and His Wonderful Limp

*This is a daring book. A book that has the nerve to put the finely crafted words of Shakespeare and Betjeman alongside the puerile offerings of Titchmarsh and friends. Three of us – Steven Alais, Robert Salter and myself – crafted this work of supreme banality to entertain a Christmas audience who, frankly, deserved better. Well, tough. Anyway, it made them laugh. And when all's said and done, we go for volume, not quality. The ability to act is a distinct disadvantage here. The ability to overact, ad lib and generally cock up, however, is essential.*

CHARACTERS

ALADDIN – the boy with the limp (male or female)
ABANAZAR – his wicked uncle
GENIE OF THE RING – a camp gentleman
CINDERELLA – a woman in tatty clothes
PUSS IN BOOTS – someone from *Cats* in tights
and whiskers
PETER PAN – a man who is older than he looks
WIDOW TWANKEE – a man in women's clothes
NARRATOR – anyone who can speak

NARRATOR: The overture, the screaming kids,
The dame in wig and corset,
Slipping feet on ice-cream lids
From Donegal to Dorset.

Its panto time for little folks,
On dirty days in Croydon,
Where dirty men crack dirty jokes
At kids that have annoyed 'em.

Come boys and girls and dads and mums,
Turn all your thoughts to rhyme,
And come and watch with all your chums
This thing called pantomime.

Abanazar, Genie, Puss,
Dame Trott, the Ugly Sisters,
Aladdin, Cinders, Mother Goose,
Oh, tell us how you missed us!

We'll fit a few into our play,
About a Chinese wimp,
Someone lively, bright and gay,
Aladdin, the boy with the limp.

•

ALADDIN: Hello boys and girls (*slaps thigh*), my name's
Aladdin! (*Slaps thigh again.*)

ABANAZAR: Little does he know that he won't be Aladdin
much longer. Ha-ha-hah! I, Abanazar, wizard and part-
time aerobics teacher, intend to bring about his demise.

ALADDIN: Hello (*slaps thigh*), who are you?

ABANAZAR: I am your uncle, my boy!

ALADDIN: I don't remember my mother talking about
her brother (*slaps thigh*). Come to that, I don't
remember her talking about her husband.

ABANAZAR: No; I'm the rottweiler of the family.

ALADDIN: The rottweiler? (*Slaps thigh.*)

ABANAZAR: Yes, it's like a black sheep, only worse.

ALADDIN: Why are you here, Uncle?

ABANAZAR: I am here to inflict my new discovery on
the world!

ALADDIN: What's that, Uncle?

ABANAZAR: The Abanazar Patent Hip and Thigh diet.

ALADDIN: But what does it do? (*Slaps thigh.*)

ABANAZAR: It makes thighs so thin and slender that even the most robust principal boy dare not slap them!

ALADDIN: Oh no! Mother, mother, where are you?

TWANKEE: Here I am dear! What's the matter with you on this merry, sunny morning in old Peking?

ALADDIN: This old man is trying to put me on a diet.

TWANKEE: A diet? My boy being starved of his food? Oooooooh! I'll not hear of it! And him with a limp, too.

ABANAZAR: Yes, but once on my diet both his thighs will become the same size and he'll never limp again!

ALADDIN: Never limp again! (*Slaps thigh.*) I'll do it, Uncle.

ABANAZAR: Then come to the cave where I have hidden my secret formula. The entrance is too small for me, but you'll be able to get at least one thigh through it.

(FX: *Jet of air indicating speed of movement … whoosh*)

ABANAZAR: Here we are, now just squeeze inside and pass me the formula. You'll find it on a shelf.

ALADDIN: (*Voice with echo*) Yes, I see it, Uncle! But Uncle, it's got someone else's name on it.

ABANAZAR: What do you mean?

ALADDIN: This book has been written by Rose-Mar-Ee Conlee, the well-known Chinese weight-watcher.

ABANAZAR: Do you know her?

ALADDIN: And she me too!

ABANAZAR: I'm not interested in her sister. Hand me the book.

ALADDIN: But there's a jewelled ring down here, too.

ABANAZAR: Leave it alone; just pass me the book.

ALADDIN: Shan't, Uncle.

ABANAZAR: Very well then; I'll leave you to your fate …
  ha-ha-haaaah!

(FX: *Stone door closing*)

ALADDIN: Oh dear, what shall I do now?

AUDIENCE: RUB THE RING!

ALADDIN: Pardon? I can't do that. Oh, very well!

(FX: *Whooshing sound*)

GENIE: Ooooh! 'Ello!

ALADDIN: Who are you?

GENIE: Ooh, don't you ever go to pantomime? I'm the
  genie of the ring, all rippling muscles and startling
  sinews.

ALADDIN: Can you get me out of here?

GENIE: Get *you* out, dear? I can't get meself out.

ALADDIN: Why's that?

GENIE: Well, I've been reading that book. Saps your
  strength good and proper it does. Now I can't move a
  muscle, let alone a whacking great stone door. Oooh,
  I'm not meself, I'm not.

ALADDIN: So what are we going to do?

GENIE: Well, you could try rubbing your limp.

ALADDIN: Rubbing my limp?

GENIE: Yes, it's a well-known fact in panto that if the principal boy rubs his limp, wonderful things happen.

ALADDIN: Like what?

GENIE: Try it and see.

ALADDIN: All right, here goes …

(FX: *Rubbing sound … whoosh*)

ALADDIN: Who's this?

GENIE: Looks like Cinderella to me. I don't think she'll be much good.

CINDERELLA: Rips in my stockings
        Holes in my frock
        Late into bed
        And up with the …

(FX: *Cockadoodledoo*)

GENIE: Oh, rub your limp again dear, she's no use.

ALADDIN: OK, here goes …

(FX: *Rubbing sound … whoosh*)

GENIE: Oh, no … Puss in Boots.

PUSS: My Lords and My Ladies
    This is a bit thick,
    Forty-two miles
    And no sign of …

GENIE: They should have that cat doctored. Get rid of him.

(FX: *Rubbing sound … whoosh*)

ALADDIN: Who's this young fella?

GENIE: He's a pain in the neck – panto's answer to Dorian Gray. He's been fighting Captain Hook for so long he's gone round the twist, and as for that girl in a nightie that he goes round with, well, she's got her own problems.

PETER PAN: Let's all get together

And kick up a shindy,

We're here at your service,

Peter Pain and Windy.

GENIE: For goodness sake, give it one last rub.

ALADDIN: It's looking a bit lacklustre.

GENIE: Like the person who's rubbing it, dear. Get on with it …

(FX: *Rubbing sound … whoosh*)

ALADDIN: Oh, no, it's Abanazar, but he's on a motorbike!

ABANAZAR: Hello me young lad,

You look smart and nifty.

How'd you like your leg over

Me Honda two-fifty!

ALADDIN: It's no good, Uncle, I haven't the strength. I've rubbed my limp so much that I simply can't lift my leg any more.

ABANAZAR: Well, why don't you go on my diet then, and all your troubles will be over?

ALADDIN: All right, Uncle, I give in, but why are you so keen for me to be slim?

ABANAZAR: The answer to your last enquiry,
On why I need a boy that's wiry,
I'll answer for you right away
To end our tale and save the day.

The fact is, lad,
Your disposition
Mucks about
With our tradition.

Whoever heard at Christmas time
About a Chinese wimp?
We loathe an oriental fool,
Especially with a limp.

And so I've come to give you this,
Please hang it in your porch,
It lights your way at Christmas time,
A solar-powered torch.

You've had the diet, slimmed your thighs
And don't look half so camp,
You'll now be known at panto time as
Aladdin and his wonderful lamp!

# The Sounds of Christmas

*F*olk who never vocalize all year (except to sing the national anthem at football and rugby internationals) can usually be counted on to join in with a carol. There can be nothing better for conjuring up the Christmas spirit, and I've peppered the words throughout the book. Carols have also inspired some of the best pieces of Christmas writing, from the likes of Laurie Lee to Kenneth Grahame.

*No self-respecting concert artiste would dream of performing without first warming up. This rhyme is useful for getting any carol singer's tongue around consonants. Say it slowly, line by line at first, and build up in speed for a mighty crescendo!*

To begin to toboggan
First buy a toboggan
But don't buy too big a toboggan.
Too big a toboggan
Is not a toboggan
To buy to begin to toboggan.

## ON CHRISTMAS NIGHT ...

On Christmas night all Christians sing,
To hear the news the angels bring;
On Christmas night all Christians sing,
To hear the news the angels bring:
News of great joy, news of great mirth,
News of our merciful King's birth.

Then why should men on earth be sad,
Since our Redeemer made us glad:
Then why should we on earth be sad,
Since our Redeemer made us glad:
When from our sin He set us free,
All for to gain our liberty.

When sin departs before Your grace,
Then life and health come in its place;
When sin departs before Your grace,
Then life and health come in its place;
Angels and men with joy may sing,
All for to see the newborn King.

All out of darkness we have light
Which made the angels sing this night;
All out of darkness we have light
Which made the angels sing this night:
'Glory to God and peace to men,
Now and forevermore. Amen.'

From CIDER WITH ROSIE
*Laurie Lee*

We approached our last house high up on the hill, the place of Joseph the farmer. For him we had chosen a special carol, which was about the other Joseph, so that we always felt that singing it added a spicy cheek to the night. The last stretch of country to reach his farm was perhaps the most difficult of all. In these rough bare lanes, open to all winds, sheep were buried and wagons lost. Huddled together, we tramped in one another's footsteps, powdered snow blew into our screwed-up eyes, the candles burnt low, some blew out altogether, and we talked loudly above the gale.

Crossing, at last, the frozen mill-stream – whose wheel in summer still turned a barren mechanism – we climbed up to Joseph's farm. Sheltered by trees, warm on its bed of snow, it seemed always to be like this. As always it was late; as always this was our final call. The snow had a fine crust upon it, and the old trees sparkled like tinsel.

We grouped ourselves round the farmhouse porch. The sky cleared, and broad streams of stars ran down over the valley and away to Wales. On Slad's white slopes, seen through the black sticks of its woods, some red lamps still burned in the windows.

Everything was quiet; everywhere there was the faint crackling silence of the winter night. We started singing, and we were all moved by the words and the sudden trueness of our voices. Pure, very clear, and breathless we sang:

As Joseph was a walking
He heard an angel sing;
'This night shall be the birth-time
Of Christ the Heavenly King.

He neither shall be bornèd
In Housen nor in hall,
Nor in a place of paradise
But in an ox's stall … '

And two thousand Christmases became real to us then; the houses, the halls, the places of paradise had all been visited; the stars were bright to guide the Kings through the snow; and across the farmyard we could hear the beasts in their stalls. We were given roast apples and hot mince-pieces, in our nostrils were spices like myrrh, and in our wooden box, as we headed back for the village, there were golden gifts for all.

# AWAY IN A MANGER

Away in a manger, no crib for a bed
The little Lord Jesus laid down His sweet head
The stars in the bright sky look down where He lay –
The little Lord Jesus asleep on the hay.

The cattle are lowing, the baby awakes
But little Lord Jesus, no crying He makes,
I love thee, Lord Jesus! Look down from the sky,
And stay by my side until morning is nigh.

Be near me, Lord Jesus; I ask thee to stay
Close by me for ever, and love me, I pray,
Bless all the dear children in Thy tender care,
And fit us for heaven to live with thee there.

*This was reputedly written by Sir Thomas Beecham when he was a child, as an offering to his father, then head of the family firm.*

## MASTER THOMAS BEECHAM'S CAROL

Hark! The herald angels sing
Beecham's pills are just the thing.
Peace on earth and mercy mild
Two for an adult, one for a child.

If you want to go to heaven
Then take five, or six, or seven;
If you want to go to hell,
Eat the ruddy box as well!

# From THE WIND IN THE WILLOWS
*Kenneth Grahame*

At last the Rat succeeded in decoying him to the table, and had just got seriously to work with the sardine-opener when sounds were heard from the fore-court without – sounds like the scuffling of small feet in the gravel and a confused murmur of tiny voices, while broken sentences reached them – 'Now, all in a line – hold the lantern up a bit, Tommy – clear your throats first – no coughing after I say one, two, three. – Where's young Bill? – Here, come on, do, we're all a-waiting –'

'What's up?' inquired the Rat, pausing in his labours.

'I think it must be the field-mice,' replied the Mole, with a touch of pride in his manner. 'They go round carol-singing regularly at this time of the year. They're quite an institution in these parts. And they never pass me over – they come to Mole End last of all; and I used to give them hot drinks, and supper too sometimes, when I could afford it. It will be like old times to hear them again.'

'Let's have a look at them!' cried the Rat, jumping up and running to the door.

It was a pretty sight, and a seasonable one, that met their eyes when they flung the door open. In the fore-court, lit by the dim rays of a horn lantern, some eight or ten little field-mice stood in a semicircle, red worsted comforters round their throats, their fore-paws thrust deep into their pockets, their feet jigging for warmth. With bright beady eyes they glanced shyly at each other, sniggering a little, sniffing and applying coat-sleeves a good deal. As the door opened, one of the elder ones that carried the lantern was just saying, 'Now then, one, two, three!' and forthwith their shrill little voices uprose on the air, singing one of the old-time carols that their forefathers composed in fields that were fallow and held by frost, or when snow-bound in chimney corners, and handed down to be sung in the miry street to lamp-lit windows at Yule time.

*Carol*
Villagers, all, this frosty tide,
Let your doors swing open wide,
Though wind may follow, and snow beside,
Yet draw us in by your fire to bide;
    Joy shall be yours in the morning!

Here we stand in the cold and the sleet,
Blowing fingers and stamping feet,
Come from far away you to greet –
You by the fire and we in the street –
    Bidding you joy in the morning!

For ere one half of the night was gone,
Sudden a star has led us on,
Raining bliss and benison –
Bliss to-morrow and more anon,
    Joy for every morning!

Goodman Joseph toiled through the snow –
Saw the star o'er a stable low;
Mary she might not further go –
Welcome thatch, and litter below!
    Joy was hers in the morning!

And then they heard the angels tell
'Who were the first to cry Nowell?
Animals all, as it befell,
In the stable where they did dwell!
    Joy shall be theirs in the morning!'

The voices ceased, the singers, bashful but smiling, exchanged sidelong glances, and silence succeeded – but for a moment only. Then, from up above and far away, down the tunnel they had so lately travelled was borne to their ears in a faint musical hum the sound of distant bells ringing a joyful and clangorous peal.

'Very well sung, boys!' cried the Rat heartily. 'And now come along in, all of you, and warm yourselves by the fire, and have something hot!'

'Yes, come along, field-mice,' cried the Mole eagerly. 'This is quite like old times! Shut the door after you. Pull up that settle to the fire. Now, you just wait a minute, while we – O, Ratty!' he cried in despair, plumping down on a seat, with tears impending. 'Whatever are we doing? We've nothing to give them!'

'You leave all that to me,' said the masterful Rat. 'Here you, with the lantern! Come over this way. I want to talk to you. Now, tell me, are there any shops open at this hour of the night?'

'Why, certainly, sir,' replied the field-mouse respectfully. 'At this time of the year our shops keep open to all sorts of hours.'

'Then look here!' said the Rat. 'You go off at once, you and your lantern, and you get me –'

Here much muttered conversation ensued, and the Mole only heard bits of it, such as – 'Fresh, mind! – no, a pound of that will do – see you get Buggins's, for I won't have any other – no, only the best – if you can't get it there, try somewhere else – yes, of course, home-made, no tinned stuff – well then, do the best you can!' Finally, there was a chink of coin passing from paw to paw, the field-mouse was provided with an ample basket for his purchases, and off he hurried, he and his lantern.

The rest of the field-mice, perched in a row on the settle, their small legs swinging, gave themselves up to enjoyment of the fire, and toasted their chilblains till they tingled; while the Mole, failing to draw them into easy conversation, plunged into family history and made each of them recite the names of his numerous brothers, who were too young, it appeared, to be allowed to go out a-carolling this year, but looked forward very shortly to winning the parental consent.

The Rat, meanwhile, was busy examining the label on one of the beer-bottles. 'I perceive this to be Old Burton,' he remarked approvingly. '*Sensible* Mole! The very thing! Now we shall be able to mull some ale! Get the things ready, Mole, while I draw the corks.'

It did not take long to prepare the brew and thrust the tin heater well into the red heart of the fire; and soon every field-mouse was sipping and coughing and choking (for a little mulled ale goes a long way) and wiping his eyes and laughing and forgetting he had ever been cold in all his life.

'They act plays too, these fellows,' the Mole explained to the Rat. 'Make them up all by themselves, and act them afterwards. And very well they do it, too! They gave us a capital one last year, about a field-mouse who was captured at sea by a Barbary corsair, and made to row in a galley; and when he escaped and got home again, his lady-love had gone into a convent. Here, *you*! You were in it, I remember. Get up and recite a bit.'

The field-mouse addressed got up on his legs, giggled shyly, looked round the room, and remained absolutely tongue-tied. His comrades cheered him on, Mole coaxed and encouraged him, and the Rat went so far as to take him by the shoulders and shake him, but nothing could overcome his stage-fright. They were all busily engaged on him like watermen applying the Royal Humane Society's regulations to a case of long sub-mersion, when the latch clicked, the door opened, and the field-mouse with the lantern reappeared, staggering under the weight of his basket.

# A CHRISTMAS CAROL

*G.K. Chesterton*

The Christ-child lay on Mary's lap,
His hair was like a light,
(O weary, weary were the world,
But here is all aright.)

The Christ-child lay on Mary's breast,
His hair was like a star.
(O stern and cunning are the kings,
But here the true hearts are.)

The Christ-child lay on Mary's heart,
His hair was like a fire.
(O weary, weary is the world,
But here the world's desire.)

The Christ-child stood at Mary's knee,
His hair was like a crown,
And all the flowers looked up at him,
And all the stars looked down.

# CAROLS IN THE ROYAL MEWS
*Alan Titchmarsh*

We'd met Alf Oates one October day at the Royal Mews when we went there as day trippers. We were eyeing up the Queen's horses and he came over, a plump, rosy-cheeked man in a green pullover with 'Royal Mews' emblazoned on the left breast.

He was one of the coachmen, and he told us stories of the Queen and her horses – nothing too indiscreet, just pleasantly amusing. As we were about to leave, he asked if we'd like to return during the week before Christmas when carols were sung to the royal horses, and Father Christmas gave out presents to the children from his sleigh. Oh, and the Queen came too, he said. We said we'd love to, and so, on Wednesday 17 December 1997, Alison, Polly, Camilla and I walked down the Mall to Buckingham Palace and entered the Royal Mews by the side gate, giving our names to the gatekeeper, who ticked us off his list. There was no posh invitation, and when we were inside the gates we were given a simple photocopied sheet with carols printed on it.

The four towering plane trees in the middle of the quadrangle were illuminated from below by red flood-lights, and there were braziers of red-hot coke glowing beneath them. The state coaches were pulled out under their glazed awnings and floodlit, and in front of the majestic golden coach, in its own stable, Lady Aldington's Singers gave their all with Christmas carols.

Alf's wife Ann met us at the gate, along with her daughter and a baby in a pushchair – her grandson. 'Alf's waiting for you,' she said, and took us over to the stable whose doors were closed. Alf stood outside, smarter today in a quilted green jacket and tie, and a flat tweed cap. 'I'll just sneak you inside,' he said, easing open the door and letting us through.

Inside the long stable, divided into pale green painted stalls with huge brass knobs atop their dividing partitions, were just two greys – Twilight and Seamus – the two that pull the Queen's coach for Trooping the Colour. Today they were to pull Father Christmas's sleigh. Their shiny black, brass-trimmed collars were being fitted by grooms, and their backs were covered with red felt blankets on to which stars and moons were stitched.

We stroked their muzzles, Twilight nipped my knuckles, hoping for a carrot, and then we went back outside to wait for Father Christmas. There were perhaps a hundred people there, and at about half past six a glistening green Jaguar purred into the quadrangle among them. No one was inside, but three people quietly ambled into the courtyard behind it: the crown equerry – an upright military gent in a buff, city-cut coat, the head coachman – also buff-coated and wearing a silk top hat, and a small, grey-haired lady in a headscarf patterned with horses, a green loden coat with cape, black trousers and black boots. She wore knitted Fair Isle gloves of cream and blue, and carried a black, patent leather handbag over her right arm.

Nobody really took much notice of the trio, who mingled with the crowd and listened to the carol singers, who were now walking towards the stables on the other side of the quadrangle. The carollers processed through the stables, singing *Hark! the Herald Angels Sing* to the horses: Kentucky and Alderney, Iceland and Monarch. The lady in the headscarf followed with her two right-hand men, part of the small crowd, now cradling in her gloved hands a white paper bag of hot roasted chestnuts.

We, and the choir and the lady in the coat, walked down one row of stalls, through a simple washroom whose notice board above a cast-iron fireplace had been decorated with pictures of the Queen and her horses. Words cut out from a newspaper – LONG MAY SHE REIGN – arched over the mantelpiece. 'I thought the crown equerry might ask me to take that down,' said Alf afterwards. 'But he didn't.'

When we emerged once more into the chill night air the distant tones of bagpipes announced the arrival of Father Christmas, who came into the courtyard on a wheeled sleigh pulled by the two greys we had patted earlier and preceded by a piper playing 'Jingle Bells'. Father Christmas was ringing a bell and waving at the children. He got out of his sleigh, sat on a raised dais equipped with a Christmas tree, and for the next hour handed out presents to the children of the Royal Household, whose names were called out through a rather dodgy microphone by the superintendent of the Royal Mews.

We had some soup from the back of a van, and some chestnuts from a brazier, roasted by the Queen's personal cook, Lionel, a portly bearded man in an anorak.

One horse, a grey right at the end of the stable, had no nameplate. 'He's new. We've been trying him out and decided he'll do,' Alf told us. 'The Queen is choosing his name tonight.'

'What do you think he'll be called?' I asked. 'Well, I've suggested two names,' said Alf.

We took our leave of Alf and Ann and the Royal Mews at about a quarter to eight, and left the last few children of the dwindling band to receive their presents from a now rather lonely Father Christmas, while others took a spin around the quadrangle in his sleigh. We didn't see the small lady with the headscarf leave. She just melted into thin air. We were told that she'd gone with the crown equerry to have a glass of sherry and pick a name for her new horse.

I rang Alf a few days later to thank him. 'It was a pleasure,' he said. And then I had to ask him: 'What did she call the horse?'

'Britannia,' said Alf, with a satisfied note in his voice. 'She called it Britannia.'

The royal yacht had been decommissioned six days earlier. The government said they couldn't afford it any more. The Queen would no longer have her Britannia. Well, that's what they thought. The Queen and Alf and me? Well, we know different.

# HARK! THE HERALD ANGELS SING

Hark! The herald angels sing,
'Glory to the newborn King;
Peace on earth, and mercy mild,
God and sinners reconciled!'
Joyful, all ye nations rise,
Join the triumph of the skies;
With th'angelic host proclaim
'Christ is born in Bethlehem!'

REFRAIN: *Hark! The herald angels sing,*
         *'Glory to the newborn King!'*

Christ, by highest heav'n adored;
Christ the everlasting Lord;
Late in time, behold Him come,
Offspring of a virgin's womb.
Veiled in flesh the Godhead see;
Hail th' incarnate Deity,
Pleased as Man with man to dwell,
Jesus our Emmanuel.

REFRAIN: *Hark! The herald angels sing,*
         *'Glory to the newborn King!'*

Hail the Heaven-born Prince of Peace!
Hail the Sun of Righteousness!
Light and life to all He brings,

Ris'n with healing in His wings.
Mild He lays His glory by,
Born that man no more may die.
Born to raise the sons of earth,
Born to give them second birth.

REFRAIN: *Hark! The herald angels sing,*
*'Glory to the newborn King!'*

## GOOD KING WENCESLAS

Good King Wenceslas looked out on the Feast of Stephen,
When the snow lay round about, deep and crisp and even.
Brightly shone the moon that night, though the frost
    was cruel,
When a poor man came in sight, gathering winter fuel.

'Hither, page, and stand by me, if you know it, telling,
Yonder peasant, who is he? Where and what his
    dwelling?'
'Sire, he lives a good league hence, underneath the
    mountain,
Right against the forest fence, by Saint Agnes' fountain.'

'Bring me food and bring me wine, bring me pine logs
    hither,

You and I will see him dine, when we bear them thither.'
Page and monarch, forth they went, forth they went
together,
Through the cold wind's wild lament and the bitter
weather.

'Sire, the night is darker now, and the wind blows
stronger,
Fails my heart, I know not how; I can go no longer.'
'Mark my footsteps, my good page, tread now in them
boldly,
You shall find the winter's rage freeze thy blood less
coldly.'

In his master's steps he trod, where the snow lay dinted;
Heat was in the very sod which the saint had printed.
Therefore, Christian men, be sure, wealth or rank
possessing,
You who now will bless the poor shall yourselves find
blessing.

## WENCESLAS: THE INSIDE STORY
*Oliver Pritchett*

'Hither,' said the page, 'and stand by me.' He was in his usual place at the end of the saloon bar with his usual pint of brown and mild in front of him. Of course, he had long since retired, but we still called him the page. He was a plump little man in a dapper double-breasted blazer and hound's-tooth trousers. His buttons, toe-caps and balding head gleamed in the firelight. He always lay in wait to corner someone and tell them about his part in the famous events which took place on the Feast of Stephen.

'Brightly shines the moon this night,' he announced.

I tried to ignore the bait and stared concentratedly at a beer mat, reading the advertising slogan on each side with exaggerated interest.

'The rude wind's lament is loud,' he said. I took the change from my pocket and counted it methodically.

'Cruel frost,' he persisted.

At last I had to relent. 'You must be the page who …'

'The very one,' he replied. You could sense his triumph as he knew he had hooked me. 'I always think about it at this time of the year when my chilblains start playing up,' he said. 'That is when I first started getting them, of course.'

'King Wenceslas must have been a very caring monarch,' I observed sagely.

'So they say.' There was something enigmatic in his tone, hinting at hidden depths and a darker secret. He was trying to lead me on. I made one more effort to frustrate him. 'Not many people in here tonight,' I said. 'Must be the bitter weather.'

The page was not going to be put off as easily as that. He squared his shoulders, raised his glass to his lips, then put it down on the bar in a portentous way.

'I have always thought there was something fishy about yonder peasant,' he said. 'It has never been satisfactorily explained what he was doing out there in the snow that night.'

'He was gathering winter's fu-el,' I replied.

'That is the official version,' said the page. 'That is what they would have us believe. But there are one or two things which do not quite fit in this story. First of all, he was not a local man, was he? If you remember, he lived a good league hence. Now that is probably about four-and-a-half miles as the crow flies. I will tell you something else peculiar. We all know that he lived underneath the mountain, right against the forest fence.' He gave me a hard meaningful stare.

'So?'

'So,' the page went on, 'if he lived right against the forest fence he had all that winter's fu-el right there on his doorstep. And if that was not enough he could always chop up the fence. So the question arises: why did he take it into his head to trek four-and-a-half miles through the snow to gather his fu-el?'

'I had never thought of that,' I confessed.

'Bit of a mystery, isn't it?'

'So there was this peasant in full view of the castle,' he went on. 'I spotted him first, as a matter of fact. I knew there would be trouble and I was just praying that King Wenceslas would not look out. I dropped a plate to distract his attention. I even told a couple of jokes. He was never much of a one for jokes. Then he happened to turn and spotted him, and he started asking all those questions. Where and what his dwelling, and all that.'

'King Wenceslas always showed an interest in the welfare of his people and in their housing conditions,' I said.

'Strictly speaking, the peasant was trespassing, of course,' the page said. 'He could have been prosecuted.'

'Good old Wenceslas was not that type,' I said.

'At the time I thought it could have been a trap. Yonder peasant could have been a terrorist from the South Bohemia Liberation Front trying to lure him outside into an ambush.'

I bought the page another brown and mild.

'Cheers, sire,' he said. Then he continued with his story. 'Actually, I think he was just a scrounger and he knew King Wenceslas was a soft touch.'

'I am sure he was needy,' I said. 'You have to remember that there was a high unemployment rate in Bohemia at that time.'

'I have always maintained,' said the page, 'that you do not solve social problems by throwing flesh and wine and pine logs at them.'

Anxious to avoid a political argument, I changed the subject. 'You obviously had a hard time, personally, getting across the fields to reach the peasant,' I said.

'Well, I was only a lad at the time. I was pretty exhausted already from bringing things hither for King Wenceslas, and, you know, the snow was not all that crisp and even. You sank in it nearly up to your knees. It was all right for Wenceslas – he was wearing nice cosy hand-stitched doe-skin boots – but all I had was a bit of sacking wrapped round my feet.'

'But he did let you step in his footprints,' I pointed out. 'Where the snow lay dinted.'

The page sighed. 'Everyone goes on about that,' he said 'What nobody seems to realise is that even at that age my feet were bigger than his. It wasn't much of a dint.'

'The thing I have always wondered about,' I said, 'is what actually happened when you got the peasant back to the castle.'

'The first thing that happened is that I retired to bed with five-day 'flu. When I got up again I found that the peasant was still there. King Wenceslas had appointed him his steward. A sort of instant job-creation scheme. He wasn't a bad fellow, really. Very efficient. Reorganised the castle's financial structure, even reduced the fu-el bill.'

The page stared glumly into his beer. 'Of course he became quite a favourite with the King. Things were never really the same after that. Everything ran very smoothly, but the atmosphere just wasn't the same. I often thought to myself: if only Wenceslas had not looked out that night.'

'I looked him up in an encyclopaedia,' I said. 'Wenceslas I mean. It said he was murdered in 929. What is the story behind that?'

The page looked uneasy. 'I wouldn't know about that,' he said. 'Nothing to do with me. He finished his drink hurriedly and made for the door. As he opened it, he buttoned up his coat and shivered. 'The night is darker now,' he said. 'And the wind blows stronger.'

THE MESSIAH (as you have never heard it!)
*A St Swithun's parishioner*

Most of us are familiar with the words and music of this great oratorio, but old Bill Jones from Golcar, a little village in the West Riding, had never been to a performance and he tried to persuade a friend to go with him to the Huddersfield Town Hall to hear the famous choral society, but his friend refused.

'Nay,' he said, 'that sort o' music's nowt in my line. I like a good comic song or a lively jig, but I reckon nowt to this sacred stuff as they call it. It's beyond me. An' another thing, there'll be none of our sort there. It'll be mostly religious folk and swells done up in boiled shirts and wimmen wi' nowt much on. Nay, you go by theesen and then you can tell me all about it sometime.'

So … Bill went by himself and the next time the old pals met, the following conversation took place.

'Well, cum on … how did you get on at *Messiah*?

'Eee, well,' said Bill, 'it were fair champion. I wouldn'ta missed it for all the tea in China. When a got there the

Town Hall were crowded, it was choc full o' folk and I had a job to get a seat, but no wonder – it was all them singers – they took up half the gallery.

'There was a chap larkin' about on the organ, he weren't playing nowt in particular, just running 'is fingers up and down as if he were practising. Well, after a bit a lot o' chaps came in carrying fiddles, then they brought in the Messiah. Well, that's what I took it to be. It were the biggest instrument on the platform and it were covered in a big green bag. Anyroad, they took the bag off it and then a bloke rubbed its belly with a stick and you should have heard it groan. It were summat like a dying cow.

'I was just thinking o' going when a little chap came on, all dolled up in a white waistcoat and wi' a flower in his buttonhole and everything went dead quiet. You could have heard a pin drop. He had a stick in his hand and he started waving it about and all the singers stared at him … I reckon they were wondering what was the matter with him.

'Then they started to sing and they hadn't been going long before they were fighting like cats. I reckon he shoulda walloped one or two of 'em with that stick. First one side said they were t'King o' Glory then t'other side said they were, and they went at it hammer and tongs, but it fizzled out, so I've no idea which side won.

'Then there was a bit of bother about some sheep that was lost. I don't know who they belonged to but one lot o' singers must have been very fond o' mutton, 'cos they kept on singing "All we like sheep". I couldn't help saying to a bloke next to me that sheep's all right in moderation, but I like a bit o' beef meself, and he looked daggers at me and said "Shhh", so I shushed.

'A lot o' wimmen stood up after that and all of 'em looked as if they were … well … gettin' on a bit. Some of 'em must a bin 64 if they was a day. They sang, "Unto us a child is born", and the chaps sang back "Wonderful", an' I thought, "Wonderful, it's a bloomin' miracle!" After that they sobered down a bit and sang about a lass called Joyce Greatly. I've never heard of her myself, but the chaps had, 'cos they all looked mighty pleased about it.

'Then some bloke got up and said he was the king o' kings, another one said he was, and then, blow me, they all started arguing about it. I was gettin' a bit fed up when everybody stood up to see what was the matter and they suddenly shouted, "Hallelujah … it's going to rain for ever and ever". Well, at that I jumped up and made straight for the door. I'd had me money's worth and besides, I was thinkin' that if it was going to rain for ever and ever, I'd better get home before the flood came.

'It was a real good do though, you shoulda come, but oh, I do hope they find them sheep.'

# Peter Pain
# and Windy

There is precious little of J.M. Barrie left in this travesty
from the pens of Titchmarsh, Salter and Alais (a gardener
and two solicitors). Once again, a peculiar talent for
acting is not at all necessary to get it across the footlights.
(A wheelbarrow might be more effective.)

CHARACTERS

PETER PAIN – a person who is older than he looks
WINDY – a scared old bird in a nightie
JOHN – her brother
MICHAEL – her other brother
CAPTAIN HOOK – a bad actor
SMEE – a bad actor's sidekick
PIRATE – an optional extra
TIGER LILY – a demure bit of stuff
MERMAID – a vamp in scales
CROCODILE – a reptile of the genus *Crocodylus*
PROLOGUE – a tall girl in tights

PROLOGUE: My Lords and My Ladies,
Stand by for some fun,
When you've finished your Birds Eye
Hot dinner for one.

It's time for our panto,
A treat is in store,
One performance with me
And you're begging for more.

It's a saga of daring
Piratical wit,

In fact you might say
It's a load of old … rubbish.

There's a mother, a father,
Two sons and a daughter,
A croc and a fairy
Who's not how she ought'ta.

There's a mermaid on shore
Who is comely and round,
Thirty-six, twenty-four,
And ten pence a pound.

We've an Indian squaw
If your taste is exotic,
She's short and she's dark,
And she aint 'alf erotic.

But the hero and villain
In our fairy-tale book,
Are the young Peter Pain,
And a bent Captain Hook.

Come with us to London,
We'll kick up a shindy,
As we tell you the tale,
Of Peter Pain and Windy.

*The nursery in the Darling home. There is a bed on stage, and Michael, Windy and John are sleeping.*

WINDY: (*Sits bolt upright.*)

> Outside our tall casement,
> Do I hear a noise?
> Oh can it be him,
> What do you think boys?
> (*Boys snore.*)
> He flies through the dawn,
> With the tits and the starlings,
> He's here, yes, he's coming …

(*Boys wake as Peter enters on large rope.*)

PETER: Hello my Darlings!

MICHAEL: I'm frightened, I'm worried,
My nerves are a-jangle,

JOHN: You'd be more upset,
If you saw him from this angle.

PETER: Now come with me, Windy,
I'm your fairy from Dover,
Hitch up your nightie,
And get your leg over.

WINDY: I'm certainly coming,
I won't make a fuss,
Can we get up together?

PETER: I'll just tighten my truss.
(FX: *Ringing of bell in wings.*)
Tonkerbell's coming,

Hear the sound of her clanger,
She's old and decrepit
But goes like a banger.
(*Windy slaps his wrist.* FX: *Ballet fairy music
as Tonkerbell – invisible except for the beam
of a torch – enters.*)
Away we all float
To our land in the skies,
Provided our ends
Don't get caught in the flies

(*Change of scene to Hardly Ever Land.*)

HOOK:    Ha-ha-ha-ha-ha!
Hello me hearties,
Me name's Captain Hook,
Ten years at the mast,
And I don't give a damn!
Shiver me timbers,
How's that for starters,
I'll have kippers for breakfast
And your guts for garters.
(*Evil laugh.*)
I am the sole ruler
Of Hardly Ever Land,
But I simply can't manage
Without me right hand.
(*Brandishes hook.*)
Splice the mainbrace,
Me wind's in the lee,

I'm needing me bosun,
The redoubtable Smee (Ne-ha-ha-ha).

SMEE: My Lords and My Ladies
This is a bit thick,
Forty-two leagues
And no sign of Dick!

HOOK: Come here me young lad,
There's no need to fidget,
Or you'll feel the length
Of me stainless-steel digit.
It's handy for whittling
And frightening your foes
But one thing is vital:
Just don't pick your nose
(FX: *Sound of flying.*)
Oh is it a bird?

|         |                                          |
|---------|------------------------------------------|
|         | Or is it a plane?                        |
|         | Oh curses, it's Tonka                    |
|         | And young Peter Pain.                    |
| SMEE:   | With three children in tow,              |
|         | To this island they fly,                 |
| HOOK:   | It makes no odds to me,                  |
|         | They'll all have to die (Ne-ha-ha-ha-ha).|
|         | The last time they came,                 |
|         | 'Twas by schooner from Chatham,          |
|         | So run up your rigging                   |
|         | And up boys and at 'em!                  |
| SMEE:   | The crew are a'coming,                   |
|         | Their ship has just docked,              |
|         | Their sabres are gleaming,               |
|         | And their weapons are cocked.            |

(*Pirates come on. Peter enters with gang. Much noise, etc.*)

| HOOK:   | Surrender you worm.                      |
| PETER:  | You're all wind and puff.                |
| HOOK:   | Shiver me timbers.                       |
| JOHN:   | Looks 'armless enough.                   |
| HOOK:   | My vengeance is swift,                   |
|         | I don't do things by halves.             |
| PETER:  | It's a wonder you're mobile at all,      |
|         | With those calves.                       |
| SMEE:   | Rely on me, Cap'n,                       |
|         | I'll soon cut their cackle,              |
|         | I'll pull out me pistols                 |
|         | And show 'em me tackle.                  |

PETER:  C'mon girls; let's give 'em 'ell!

WINDY: (*Hands on hips*)

Just leave it to us, Pete,
We'll cut them to size;
If he comes near me,
Then I'll scratch out his eyes.

PIRATE: (*Letting out blood-curdling yell*)

So let's up and at 'em;
We'll tear 'em asunder,
We'll prove that we pirates
Are all blood and thunder!

(*Hook leaps into Smee's arms, John leaps into Michael's, and Peter into Windy's. Then staged fight to music.*)

PETER:  There's no one left, Hook,
To answer your call;
You'll be incarcerated,

HOOK:  The worst cut of all.
At your jibes and your jests
I will sneer and I'll scoff,
But having said that,
I think I'll push off.

(*Exit*)

SMEE:  I'm armed to the teeth,
All sinew and bone,
Hardly Ever Land's answer
To Sylvester Stallone.

PETER:  You can't fool with me, Smee,

With your whiskers and tat,
Underneath you look more like
Sylvester the cat.

MICHAEL: One captain

JOHN: His henchman

PETER: We've managed to conquer;

WINDY: I'm feeling quite stiff,

JOHN: But look at poor Tonka.

(*Weak torch beam on floor.*)

PETER: To breathe life in that body
She needs a good clap;
So do it for me;
I'm a nice little chap.
Come on, boys and girls,
Johnnys, Dicks, Toms and Marys;
Tell me right now
Do you believe in fairies?

(*Beam starts to move rapidly. Plaintive cries from wings.*)

JOHN: But hark, over there,
I can hear some strange things;

WINDY: I'll just wander off
For a peek in the wings.

JOHN: I'd like one, too,
It will make me feel gladder,
All this excitement
Has weakened my bladder.

(*John crosses his legs and runs. Michael does the same.*)

WINDY:    Look who we found
             All fussed and forlorn,
             Their spirits are tattered,
             Their clothes are all torn.

PETER:    I've seen her before,
             Her name's Tiger Lily;
             She's a sensitive flower

(*John gooses her with his teddy.*)

TIGER LILY: Oooh!

PETER:    No; don't be so silly.
             And that's Bubbles the mermaid,
             She's comely and dishy,
             She glints in the sun

JOHN: (*Nose in the mermaid's navel*)
             But she smells a bit fishy.

MICHAEL: (*Pointing and looking down*)
             'Ere look at 'er,
             She ain't got no feet.

PETER:    Just cast your eyes higher,

MICHAEL:  Ooooh! Ain't they a treat!

TIGER LILY: I'm distraught and upset,
             Uncontrollably weepy,
             On account of the things
             That Hook did in my tepee.

MERMAID:  I was sick to the gills
             When with Hook I was billeted;

|          | I've been smoked and descaled |
|          | And unpleasantly filleted. |
| HOOK: | I'll swing into sight |
|          | On this trusty old rope; |
|          | I'll have you tonight |
| PETER: | Oooh, you've got some 'ope! |

(*Smee and Pirate enter, panting.*)

| SMEE: | All right, I give in, |
|          | I've sheathed my stiletto; |
|          | Instead I'll lick lollies |
|          | And suck me Cornetto. |
| HOOK: | I'm putting a stop |
|          | To your juvenile pranks. |
| PETER: | Your weapon is useless, |
|          | It's loaded with blanks. |

(*Hook fires blank shot.*)

| HOOK: | Aaargh! |
| PETER: | The game is up Hook, |
|          | Discard your utensil, |
|          | It's proved once and for all |
|          | There's no lead in your pencil. |
| HOOK: | Thwarted again, |
|          | By my halyard I'm hoisted, |
|          | I've failed for the last time, |
|          | With fate I am foisted. |

*(Crocodile enters during previous verse – hopefully to audience shouts of 'Look out; behind you', etc.)*

HOOK:      My Lords and My Ladies,
I'm shaken and shocked;
For your old Captain Hook
Has been finally crocked!

*(Crocodile gets Hook.)*

WINDY:     The moral of this story is,
When all your hopes are pinned up;
Don't turn your back on a crocodile
Or you will get the wind up.

*(Windy bows.)*

PETER:     So remember when you're losing,
And fate has played a trick,
However sharp and large the hook,
It's just a little prick.

*(All bow.)*

CURTAIN

# Christmas Presents

*Either you start early – buying them back in September – of you do what dads do and nip to the shops on Christmas Eve. In a perfect world you'll split the difference and get the choice absolutely right. And nobody will buy you socks.*

# A LETTER TO ST NICK
*Alan Titchmarsh*

Dear Father Christmas, please be kind
And leave me lots of stuff behind.

I'd like a bike but I won't fret
If all I get's a painting set.

It's all the rest that live here, too,
That need some bits and bobs from you.

Like Dad, who says he likes Old Spice,
Please! CK One is twice as nice.

For Mum, whose nails are varnished red,
Please send her some pale blue instead.

My brother has a room that stinks
Although it's trendy (so he thinks)

To wear the same clothes every day.
Send soap to take the smell away.

My sister, the last of the really big spenders,
Loves that young guy off *EastEnders*.

Send her his poster, Santa, do,
And one for me – I love him, too!

There's just two more who need a treat
Although they're old with aching feet:

Gran and Grandad end my list.
By now I think you've got the gist.

Send Granny chocolates – she's on a diet.
Grandad? He just wants peace and quiet.

Whatever else the season brings,
I hope that you get some nice things.

'Cos just like socks don't make Dad merry,
You must be really sick of sherry.

# A VISIT FROM ST NICHOLAS
*Clement Clark Moore*

'Twas the night before Christmas, when all through
  the house
Not a creature was stirring, not even a mouse;
The stockings were hung by the chimney with care,
In hopes that St Nicholas soon would be there;
The children were nestled all snug in their beds,
While visions of sugar-plums danced in their heads;
And mamma in her 'kerchief, and I in my cap,
Had just settled our brains for a long winter's nap,
When out on the lawn there arose such a clatter,
I sprang from the bed to see what was the matter.
Away to the window I flew like a flash,
Tore open the shutters and threw up the sash.
The moon on the breast of the new-fallen snow
Gave the lustre of mid-day to objects below,
When, what to my wondering eyes should appear,
But a miniature sleigh, and eight tiny reindeer,
With a little old driver, so lively and quick,
I knew in a moment it must be St Nick.
More rapid than eagles his coursers they came,
And he whistled, and shouted, and called them by name;
'Now Dasher! now, Dancer! now, Prancer and Vixen!
On, Comet! on, Cupid! on, Donner and Blitzen!
To the top of the porch! to the top of the wall!
Now dash away! dash away! dash away all!'
As dry leaves that before the wild hurricane fly,
When they meet with an obstacle, mount to the sky,

So up to the house-top the coursers they flew,
With the sleigh full of toys, and St Nicholas too.
And then, in a twinkling, I heard on the roof
The prancing and pawing of each little hoof.
As I drew in my head, and was turning around,
Down the chimney St Nicholas came with a bound.
He was dressed all in fur, from his head to his foot,
And his clothes were all tarnished with ashes and soot.
A bundle of toys he had flung on his back,
And he looked like a pedlar, just opening his pack.
His eyes – how they twinkled! his dimples how merry!
His cheeks were like roses, his nose like a cherry!
His droll little mouth was drawn up like a bow,
And the beard of his chin was as white as the snow;
The stump of a pipe he held tight in his teeth,
And the smoke it encircled his head like a wreath;
He had a broad face and a little round belly,
That shook when he laughed, like a bowlful of jelly.
He was chubby and plump, a right jolly old elf,
And I laughed when I saw him, in spite of myself;
A wink of his eye and a twist of his head,
Soon gave me to know I had nothing to dread.
He spoke not a word, but went straight to his work,
And filled all the stockings; then turned with a jerk,
And laying his finger aside of his nose,
And giving a nod, up the chimney he rose;
He sprang to his sleigh, to his team gave a whistle,
And away they all flew like the down of a thistle.
But I heard him exclaim, 'ere he drove out of sight,
'Happy Christmas to all, and to all a good-night.'

*If Christmas seems to have lost its magic over the years, maybe this verse will strike a chord with you. It certainly does with this father of two daughters.*

## ALL THE DAYS OF CHRISTMAS
*Phyllis McGinley*

What shall my true love
Have from me
To pleasure his Christmas
Wealthily?
The partridge has flown
From our pear tree.

Flown with our summers,
Are the swans and the geese.
Milkmaids and drummers
Would leave him little peace.
I've no gold ring
And no turtle dove.
So what can I bring
To my true love?

A coat for the drizzle,
Chosen at the store;
A saw and a chisel
For mending the door;
A pair of red slippers

To slip on his feet;
Three striped neckties;
Something sweet.

He shall have all
I can best afford –
No pipers, piping,
No leaping lord,
But a fine fat hen
For his Christmas board;
Two pretty daughters
(Versed in the role)
To be worn like pinks
In his buttonhole;
And the tree of my heart
With its calling linnet,
My evergreen heart
And the bright bird in it.

*I have already been rude about socks, but some folks will be perfectly happy with a pair as their present. I have one faithful fan who sends me a designer hanky every Christmas, and I look forward to it arriving. Honestly. You see, I've never been much of a tissue man. But the very best presents of all are those that are home-made and from those who put precious time into showing how much they care. The following story by Keith Waterhouse is my all-time favourite.*

## ALBERT AND THE LINER
*Keith Waterhouse*

Below the military striking clock in the City Arcade there was, and for all I know still is, a fabulous toyshop.

It was a magic grotto, that shop. A zoo, a circus, a pantomime, a travelling show, a railway exhibition, an enchanting public library, a clockwork museum, an archive of boxed games, a pavilion of sports equipment, a depository of all the joys of the indefinite, endless leisure of the winter holiday – but first, the military striking clock.

Once a year we were taken to see the clock strike noon – an event in our lives as colourful, and traditional, and as fixed and immovable in the calendar of pageantry as Trooping the Colour. Everybody who was anybody assembled, a few minutes before twelve, on the patch of worn tiles incorporating an advertisement for tomato sausages done in tasteful mosaic, beneath that military striking clock.

There was me, and Jack Corrigan, and the crippled lad from No. 43, and there was even Albert Skinner – whose father never took him anywhere, not even to the Education Office to explain why he'd been playing truant.

Albert Skinner, with his shaved head and his shirt-lap hanging out of his trousers, somehow attached himself, insinuated himself, like a stray dog. You'd be waiting at the tram stop with your mother, all dolled up in your Sunday clothes for going into town and witnessing the ceremony of the military striking clock, and Albert, suddenly, out of nowhere, would be among those present.

'Nah, then, kid.'

And your mother, out of curiosity, would say – as she was meant to say – 'You're never going into town looking like that, are you, Albert?'

And Albert would say: 'No. I was, only I've lost my tram fare.'

And your mother, out of pity, would say – as she was meant to say – 'Well, you can come with us. But you'll have to tidy yourself up. Tuck your shirt in, Albert.'

So at Christmastime Albert tagged on to see the military striking clock strike noon. And after the mechanical soldiers of the King had trundled back into their plaster-of-Paris garrison, he, with the rest of us, was allowed to press his nose to the fabulous toyshop window.

Following a suitable period of meditation, we were then treated to a bag of mint imperials – 'and think on, they're to share between you' – and conveyed home on the rattling tram. And there, thawing out our mottled legs by the fireside, we were supposed to compose our petitions to Father Christmas.

Dear Father Christmas, for Christmas I would like …

'Don't know what to put,' we'd say at length to one another, seeking some kind of corporate inspiration.

'Why don't you ask him for a sledge? I am.'

'Barmpot, what do you want a sledge for? What if it doesn't snow?'

'Well – a cricket bat and stumps, and that.'

'Don't play cricket at Christmas, barmpot.'

Albert Skinner said nothing. Nobody, in fact, said anything worth saying during those tortured hours of voluntary composition.

With our blank jumbo jotters on our knees, we would suck our copying-ink pencils until our tongues turned purple – but it wasn't that we were short of ideas. Far from it: sledges, cricket bats with stumps and that, fountain pens, dynamos, cinematographs complete with Mickey Mouse films – the fact of the matter was, there was too much choice.

For the fabulous toyshop, which sparked off our exotic and finally blank imaginations, was the nearest thing on this earth to Santa's Workshop. It was like a bankruptcy sale in heaven. The big clockwork train ran clockwise and the small electric train ran anti-clockwise, and there was Noah's Ark, and a tram conductor's set, and a junior typewriter revolving on a brightly lit glass shelf, and a fairy cycle hanging from the ceiling on invisible wires, and a tin steam roller, and the *Tip-Top Annual* and the *Film Fun Annual* and the *Radio Fun*

*Annual* and the *Jingles Annual* and the *Joker Annual* and the *Jester Annual*, and board games, and chemistry sets, and conjuring sets, and carpentry sets – everything, in short, that the modern boy would give his eyeteeth for.

Everything that Albert Skinner would have given his eye-teeth for, in fact, and much that Albert Skinner would never get. And not only him. There were items that no reasonable modern boy expected to find in his Christmas pillow-case – not even though he bartered every tooth in his head and promised to be a good lad till kingdom come.

The centrepiece of the fabulous toyshop's window display was always something that was out of the reach of ordinary mortals, such as the Blackpool Tower in Meccano, or a mechanical carousel with horses that went up and down on their brass poles like the real thing, or Windsor Castle made of a million building bricks, or Buckingham Palace with knobs on – floodlit. None of us had to be told that such luxuries were beyond Father Christmas's price range.

This year the window featured a splendid model of the *Queen Mary*, which had recently been launched on Clydebank. It was about four feet long, with real lights in the portholes, real steam curling out of the funnels, and a crew, and passengers, and lifeboats, and cabin trunks, all to scale – and clearly it was not for the likes of us.

Having seen it and marvelled at it, we dismissed this expensive dream from our minds, sucked our copying-ink pencils and settled down to list our prosaic requests –

for Plasticine, for farmyard animals that poisoned you when you licked the paint off, and for one pair of roller skates between two of us.

All of us, that is to say, except Albert Skinner. Having considered several possibilities, and taken advice on the rival merits of a racing track with eight electric sports cars and a glove puppet of Felix the Cat he'd rather fancied, Albert calmly announced that he'd given thought to all our suggestions and he was asking Father Christmas for the *Queen Mary*.

This, as you might imagine, was greeted with some scepticism.

'What – that one in the Arcade window? With all the lights and the steam coming out and that? You've never asked for that, have you?'

'Yeh – course I have. Why shouldn't I?'

'He's blinking crackers. Hey, Skinno, why don't you ask for them soldiers that march in and out and bang that clock? Because you've more chance of getting them than that *Queen Mary*.'

'If I'd wanted them soldiers, I'd have asked for them. Only I don't. So I've asked him for the *Queen Mary*.'

'Who – Father Christmas?'

'No – him on the Quaker Oats Box, who do you think?'

'Bet you haven't, man. Bet you're having us on.'

'I'm not – God's honour. I've asked him for the *Queen Mary*.'

'Let's see the letter, then.'

'Can't – I've chucked it up the chimney.'

'Yeh – bet you have. Anyway, your dad won't get it for you – he can't afford it.'

'What's it got to do with him? I'm asking Father Stinking Rotten Christmas for it, not me dad. Dozy.'

'What else have you asked for, Skinno?'

'Nowt. I don't want owt else. I just want the *Queen Mary*. And I'm getting it, as well.'

Little else was said at the time, but privately we thought Albert was a bit of an optimist. For one thing, the *Queen Mary* was so big and so grand and so lit up that it was probably not even for sale. For another, we were all well aware that Father Christmas's representative in the Skinner household was a sullen, foul-tempered collier who also happened to be unemployed.

Albert's birthday present, it was generally known, had been a pair of boots – instead of the scooter on which, at that time, he had set his heart.

Even so, Albert continued to insist that he was getting the *Queen Mary* for Christmas. 'Ask my dad,' he would say. 'If you don't believe me, ask my dad.'

None of us cared to broach the subject with the excitable Mr Skinner. But sometimes, when we went to his house to swap comics, Albert would raise the matter himself.

'Dad, I am, aren't I? Aren't I, Dad? Getting that *Queen Mary* for Christmas?'

Mr Skinner, dourly whittling a piece of wood by the fireside after the habit of all the local miners, would growl without looking up: 'You'll get a clout over the bloody earhole if you don't stop chelping.'

Albert would turn complacently to us. 'I am, see. I'm getting the *Queen Mary*. Aren't I, Dad? Dad? Aren't I?'

Sometimes, when his father had come home from the pub in a bad mood (which was quite often), Albert's pleas for reassurance would be met with a more vicious response. 'Will you shut up about the bloody *Queen swining Mary*!' Mr Skinner would shout. 'You gormless little git, do you think I'm made of money?'

Outside, his ear tingling from the blow his father had landed on it, Albert would bite back the tears and declare stubbornly: 'I'm still getting it. You wait till Christmas.'

Christmas Eve was but a fortnight off by then. Most of us had a shrewd idea, from hints dropped by our mothers, what Father Christmas would be bringing us – or, in most cases, not bringing. 'I don't think Father Christmas can manage an electric train set this year, our

Terry. He says they're too expensive. He says he might be able to find you a tip-up lorry.'

Being realists, we accepted our lowly position on Father Christmas's scale of priorities – and we tried our best to persuade Albert to accept his.

'You're not *forced* to get that *Queen Mary*, you know, Skinno.'

'Who says I'm not?'

'My mam. She says it's too big to go in Father Christmas's sack.'

'Yeh, well, that's all *she* knows. Because he's fetching Jacky Corrigan a fairy cycle – so if he can't get the *Queen Mary* in his sack, how can he get a stinking rotten fairy cycle?'

'Yeh, well he isn't fetching me a fairy cycle at all, clever clogs, he's fetching me a John Bull printing outfit. 'Cos he told my mam.'

'I don't care what he told her, or what he didn't tell her. He's still fetching me that *Queen Mary*.'

The discussion was broken up by the sudden appearance of Mr Skinner at their scullery window. 'If I hear one more bloody word from you about that bloody *Queen Mary*, you'll get nothing for Christmas! Do you hear me?' And there the matter rested.

A few days later the crippled lad at No. 43 was taken by the Church Ladies Guild to see the military striking clock in the City Arcade, and when he came home he reported that the model of the *Queen Mary* was no longer in the window of the fabulous toyshop.

'I know,' said Albert, having confirmed that his father was out of earshot. 'I'm getting it for Christmas.'

And, indeed, it seemed the only explanation possible. The fabulous toyshop never changed its glittering display until after Boxing Day – it was unheard of. Some minor item might vanish out of the window – the Noah's Ark, perhaps, or a farmyard, or a game of Monopoly or two. There was a rational explanation for this: Father Christmas hadn't enough toys to go round and he'd been obliged, so to speak, to call on his sub-contractors. But the set-piece, the Blackpool Tower made out of Meccano or the carousel with the horses that went round and round and up and down – that was never removed; never. And yet the *Queen Mary* had gone. What had happened? Had Father Christmas gone mad? Had Mr Skinner bribed him – and if so, with what? Had Mr Skinner won the football pools? Or was it that Albert's unswerving faith could move mountains – not to mention ocean-going liners with real steam and real lights in the portholes? Or was it, as one cynic among us insisted, that the *Queen Mary* had been privately purchased for some pampered grammar school lad on the posher side of town?

'You just wait and see,' said Albert.

And then it was Christmas morning; and after the chocolate pennies had been eaten and all the kitchens in the street were awash with nut-shells and orange peel, we all flocked out to show off our presents – sucking our brand-new torches to make our cheeks glow red, or brandishing a lead soldier or two in the pretence that we had a whole regiment of them indoors. Those who had wanted wooden forts were delighted with their painting books; those who had prayed for electric racing cars were content with their Dinky toys; those who had asked for roller skates were happy with their pencil boxes; and there was no sign of Albert.

No one, in fact, expected to see him at all. But just as we were asking each other what Father Christmas could have brought him – a new jersey, perhaps, or a balaclava helmet – he came bounding, leaping, jumping, almost somersaulting into the street. 'I've got it! I've got it! I've got it!'

Painting books and marbles and games of Happy Families were abandoned in the gutter as we clustered around Albert, who was cradling in his arms what seemed on first inspection to be a length of wood. Then we saw that it had been roughly carved at both ends, to make a bow and a stern, and that three cotton-reels had been nailed to it for funnels. A row of tintacks marked the Plimsoll line, and there were stuck-on bits of cardboard for portholes. The whole thing was painted over in sticky lamp-black, except for the lettering on the portside.

'*The Queen Mary*,' it said. In white, wobbling letters. Capital T, small h, capital E. Capital Q, small u, capital E, capital E, small n. Capital M, small a, capital R, small y. Penmanship had never been Mr Skinner's strong point.

'See!' crowed Albert complacently. 'I told you he'd fetch me it, and he's fetched me it.'

Our grunts of appreciation, though somewhat strained, were genuine enough. Albert's *Queen Mary* was a crude piece of work, but clearly many hours of labour, and much love, had gone into it. Its clumsy contours alone must have taken night after night of whittling by the fireside.

Mr Skinner, pyjama jacket tucked into his trousers, had come out of the house and was standing by his garden gate. Albert, in a rush of happiness, ran to his father and flung his arms around him and hugged him. Then he waved the *Queen Mary* on high.

'Look, Dad! Look what I've got for Christmas! Look what Father Christmas has fetched me! You knew he would, didn't you, all this time!'

'Get out of it, you soft little bugger,' said Mr Skinner. He drew contentedly on his empty pipe, cuffed Albert over the head as a matter of habit, and went indoors.

From LITTLE WOMEN
*Louisa May Alcott*

Jo was the first to wake in the grey dawn of Christmas morning. No stockings hung at the fireplace, and for a moment she felt as much disappointed as she did long ago, when her little sock fell down because it was so crammed with goodies. Then she remembered her mother's promise, and, slipping her hand under her pillow, drew out a little crimson-covered book. She knew it very well, for it was that beautiful old story of the best life ever lived, and Jo felt that it was a true guide-book for any pilgrim going the long journey. She woke Meg with a 'Merry Christmas', and bade her see what was under her pillow. A green-covered book appeared, with the same picture inside, and a few words written by their mother, which made their one present very precious in their eyes. Presently Beth and Amy woke, to rummage and find their little books also – one dove-coloured, the other blue; and all sat looking at and talking about them, while the east grew rosy with the coming day.

# TOYS AND TANGERINES
*Dylan Thomas*

There were the Useful Presents: engulfing mufflers of the old coach days, and mittens made for giant sloths; zebra scarves of a substance like silky gum that could be tug-o'-warred down to the galoshes; blinding tam-o'-shanters like patchwork tea cosies and bunny-suited busbies and balaclavas for victims of head-shrinking tribes; from aunts who always wore wool next to the skin there were moustached and rasping vests that made you wonder why the aunts had any skin left at all; and once I had a little crocheted nose bag from an aunt now, alas, no longer whinnying with us. And pictureless books in which small boys, though warned with quotations not to, *would* skate on Farmer Giles' pond and did and drowned; and books that told me everything about the wasp, except why.

*List who gave you what as you open your presents or you'll never remember. And don't wait more than a week before writing thank-you letters. Well, that's what my mum said.*

## CHRISTMAS THANK YOUS
*Mick Gowar*

Dear Auntie
Oh, what a nice jumper
I've always adored powder blue
and fancy you thinking of
orange and pink
for the stripes
how clever of you!

Dear Uncle
The soap is
terrific
So
useful
and such a kind thought and
how did you guess that
I'd just used the last of
the soap that last Christmas brought?

Dear Gran
Many thanks for the hankies
Now I really can't wait for the flu
and the daisies embroidered
in red round the 'M'
for Michael

how
thoughtful of you!

Dear Cousin
What socks!
and the same sort you wear
so you must be
the last word in style
and I'm certain you're right that the
luminous green
*will* make me stand out a mile.

Dear Sister
I quite understand your concern
it's a risk sending jam in the post
But I think I've pulled out
all the big bits
of glass
so it won't taste too sharp
spread on toast.

Dear Grandad
Don't fret
I'm delighted
So *don't* think your gift will
offend
I'm not at all hurt
that you gave up this year
and just sent me
a fiver
to spend.

# THE TWELVE DAYS OF CHRISTMAS

On the first day of
   Christmas,
My true love sent to me
A partridge in a
   pear tree.

On the second day of
   Christmas,
My true love sent to me
Two turtle doves,
And a partridge in a
   pear tree.

On the third day of
   Christmas,
My true love sent to me
Three French hens,
Two turtle doves,
And a partridge in a
   pear tree.

On the fourth day of
   Christmas,
My true love sent to me
Four calling birds,
Three French hens,
Two turtle doves,
And a partridge in a
   pear tree.

On the fifth day of
   Christmas,
My true love sent to me
Five golden rings,
Four calling birds,
Three French hens,
Two turtle doves,
And a partridge in a
   pear tree.

On the sixth day of
   Christmas,
My true love sent to me
Six geese a-laying,
Five golden rings,
Four calling birds,
Three French hens,
Two turtle doves,
And a partridge in a
   pear tree.

On the seventh day of
   Christmas,
My true love sent to me
Seven swans a-swimming,
Six geese a-laying,
Five golden rings,
Four calling birds,
Three French hens,
Two turtle doves,
And a partridge in a
   pear tree.

On the eighth day of
   Christmas,
My true love sent to me
Eight maids a-milking,
Seven swans a-swimming,
Six geese a-laying,

Five golden rings,
Four calling birds,
Three French hens,
Two turtle doves,
And a partridge in a
   pear tree.

On the ninth day of
   Christmas,
My true love sent to me
Nine ladies dancing,
Eight maids a-milking,
Seven swans a-swimming,
Six geese a-laying,
Five golden rings,
Four calling birds,
Three French hens,
Two turtle doves,
And a partridge in a
   pear tree.

On the tenth day of
   Christmas,
My true love sent to me
Ten lords a-leaping,
Nine ladies dancing,
Eight maids a-milking,
Seven swans a-swimming,
Six geese a-laying,

Five golden rings,
Four calling birds,
Three French hens,
Two turtle doves,
And a partridge in a
    pear tree.

On the eleventh day of
    Christmas,
My true love sent to me
Eleven pipers piping,
Ten lords a-leaping,
Nine ladies dancing,
Eight maids a-milking,
Seven swans a-swimming,
Six geese a-laying,
Five golden rings,
Four calling birds,
Three French hens,
Two turtle doves,

And a partridge in a
    pear tree.

On the twelfth day of
    Christmas,
My true love sent to me
Twelve drummers
    drumming,
Eleven pipers piping,
Ten lords a-leaping,
Nine ladies dancing,
Eight maids a-milking,
Seven swans a-swimming,
Six geese a-laying,
Five golden rings,
Four calling birds,
Three French hens,
Two turtle doves,
And a partridge in a
    pear tree.

# Politically Correct Snow White

*by Alan Titchmarsh*

---

*Time was when the Lord Chamberlain could descend on a West End play and insist on cuts in the dialogue in the interests of common decency. For the last 50 years such censorship has disappeared from our lives, but you may have noticed that recently there has been a move towards political correctness, which once again threatens our freedom of speech. It can only be a matter of time before the Ministry of Political Correctness imposes its own form of censorship on the simplest forms of entertainment …*

CHARACTERS

THE NARRATOR – well-spoken and even-tempered
(under normal circumstances)
MINISTRY MAN 1 – particularly strict in the application
of rules
MINISTRY MAN 2 – his sidekick

NARRATOR: Once upon a time there was a large wood.
And in the middle of the wood was a small cottage.
Within that cottage lived a fair young maiden by the
name of Snow White. And she did not live alone. With
her lived seven dwarfs, and their names were Happy,
Dopey, Sleepy, Sneezy, Bashful, Grumpy and Doc.

MINISTRY MAN 1: (*Pushing his way on to the stage with
Ministry Man 2*) Excuse me! Excuse me!

NARRATOR: Yes?

MINISTRY MAN 1: Are you licensed for this production?

NARRATOR: I'm sorry?

MINISTRY MAN 1: You have to have a licence to perform
this sort of work.

MINISTRY MAN 2: Oh, yes. A licence. (*He holds up a paper.*)

NARRATOR: What sort of licence?

MINISTRY MAN 1: A licence from the Ministry of Political
Correctness.

NARRATOR: Never heard of it.

MINISTRY MAN 1: Well, that's no excuse.

MINISTRY MAN 2: No excuse at all.

MINISTRY MAN 1: Where would we be if folk like you simply flouted the regulations willy nilly?

MINISTRY MAN 2: Willy nilly.

MINISTRY MAN 1: Precisely.

NARRATOR: Well, what am I meant to do?

MINISTRY MAN 1: Well, since you haven't submitted your script …

MINISTRY MAN 2: In triplicate …

MINISTRY MAN 1: … we'll just have to vet it as we go.

NARRATOR: I see.

MINISTRY MAN 1: We'll sit here (*they sit on chairs at the side of the stage*) and we'll ring this bell (*produces bell from bag*) when we want to make a change.

NARRATOR: (*Looking nervous*) Right. Shall I start again?

MINISTRY MAN 1: If you would.

MINISTRY MAN 2: We don't want to miss anything.

NARRATOR: Once upon a time … (*glances at the men from the Ministry*) Am I all right so far?

MINISTRY MAN 1: Perfectly fine. We have no problem with that, do we?

MINISTRY MAN 2: No problem at all.

NARRATOR: Good. Once upon a time there was a large wood. (*He looks at the men who show no reaction. Emboldened, he continues.*) And in the middle of the wood was a small house. (*Ministry Man 1 rings bell*) Yes?

MINISTRY MAN 2: Was this green belt land?

NARRATOR: I don't know. Why?

MINISTRY MAN 1: Did they have planning permission?

NARRATOR: What?

MINISTRY MAN 2: For the house. There's something called the Gummer Clause, which allows you to build a house in the middle of a large patch of meadow or woodland, but only if it is of significant architectural merit.

MINISTRY MAN 1: Do you think the house was of significant architectural merit?

NARRATOR: It was a cottage.

MINISTRY MAN 1: Unlikely then. In which case, we suggest your cottage was in the middle of a housing estate.

MINISTRY MAN 2: Yes, much more likely.

NARRATOR: Fine. Once upon a time there was a large housing estate. And in the middle of the housing estate was a small cottage. Within that cottage lived a fair young maiden by the name of Snow White.

*(Bell rings. Narrator looks at the Ministry Men who shake their heads in unison. Narrator shakes his head.)*

MINISTRY MAN 1 AND MINISTRY MAN 2: No, no, no, no, no.

NARRATOR: No?

MINISTRY MAN 1 AND MINISTRY MAN 2: No.

NARRATOR: What then? This is the essence of the story.

MINISTRY MAN 1: Yes, but it could be offensive.

NARRATOR: To who?

MINISTRY MAN 1: Ethnic minorities.

NARRATOR: I see.

MINISTRY MAN 1: What we need is a name that is suitably neutral.

MINISTRY MAN 2: Neutral. Yes.

MINISTRY MAN 1: You see, it would be equally offensive if she were called Rose Red.

MINISTRY MAN 2: Don't want to upset the communists.

(*Ministry Man 1 and Ministry Man 2 consult.*)

MINISTRY MAN 1: We suggest that she's called Olive Brown.

NARRATOR: Olive Brown?

MINISTRY MAN 2: Happy medium.

NARRATOR: (*A little irritably*) Within that cottage lived a fair young maiden by the name of Olive Brown.

MINISTRY MAN 1: (*Rings bell*) Does she have to be young?

NARRATOR: Sorry?

MINISTRY MAN 2: Ageist.

MINISTRY MAN 1: May we suggest a maiden of indeterminate years?

NARRATOR: Within that cottage lived a maiden of indeterminate years by the name of Olive Brown. And she did not live alone.

MINISTRY MAN 1: (*To Ministry Man 2*) Perfectly fine as long as she paid her council tax.

NARRATOR: With her lived seven dwarfs …

(*Ministry Man 1 rings bell long and loud.*)

MINISTRY MAN 2: Good heavens!

NARRATOR: No?

MINISTRY MAN 1 AND MINISTRY MAN 2: Oh dear, no.
Vertically challenged persons.

NARRATOR: I suppose I should have seen that one coming. With her lived seven vertically challenged persons, and their names were Happy, Dopey, Sleepy, Sneezy, Bashful, Grumpy and Doc.

(*Ministry Man 1 rings bell.*)

MINISTRY MAN 2: Can we take those one at a time?

NARRATOR: Happy?

MINISTRY MAN 1: Fine. No problem with that.

NARRATOR: (*Brightening*) Oh, right. Happy, Dopey …

MINISTRY MAN 1: Oh, no, no, no.

MINISTRY MAN 2: Not very encouraging, is it? Have you any idea how many problems we have with the education system, without you making things worse?

NARRATOR: (*Testily*) What then?

(*Ministry Man 1 and Ministry Man 2 confer.*)

MINISTRY MAN 1: We suggest Special Needsy.

NARRATOR: (*Sarcastically*) And their names were Happy, Special Needsy, Sleepy, Sneezy …

MINISTRY MAN 1: (*Rings bell*) He was probably just hypo-allergenic.

NARRATOR: Happy, Special Needsy, Sleepy, Hypo-allergenic, Bashful, Grumpy and …

MINISTRY MAN 1: (*Rings bell*) How grumpy?

NARRATOR: (*With feeling*) Very grumpy!

MINISTRY MAN 2: (*Shaking head*) Dangerous.

MINISTRY MAN 1: Very dangerous. Never know what it could lead to.

(*Ministry Man 1 and Ministry Man 2 confer.*)

MINISTRY MAN 2: Can we suggest ASBO?

NARRATOR: And their names were Happy, Special Needsy, Sleepy, Hypo-allergenic, Bashful, ASBO and Doc.

(*Ministry Man 1 rings bell.*)

MINISTRY MAN 2: Have you any idea of the pressure on the health service today?

NARRATOR: (*Suppressing anger*) I'm getting there.

MINISTRY MAN 1: To suggest that we have enough doctors to put one in every house of eight people is just stretching credibility to the extreme.

NARRATOR: What then?

(*Ministry Man 1 and Ministry Man 2 confer.*)

MINISTRY MAN 1: You could have a paramedic.

NARRATOR: Once upon a time there was a large housing estate. In the middle of the housing estate was a small cottage. In that cottage lived a maiden of indeterminate years by the name of Olive Brown. And she did not live alone. With her lived seven vertically challenged persons, and their names were Happy, Special Needsy, Sleepy, Hypo-allergenic, Bashful, ASBO and Paramedic.

MINISTRY MAN 1: Great story.

MINISTRY MAN 2: Very enjoyable. Do go on.

NARRATOR: Each day, the seven vertically challenged persons went to work down the mine.

MINISTRY MAN 1: (*Rings bell*) Not any more.

MINISTRY MAN 2: Mrs Thatcher saw to that.

NARRATOR: What then?

(*Ministry Man 1 and Ministry Man 2 confer.*)

MINISTRY MAN 1: We suggest that they could work in advertising and PR.

MINISTRY MAN 2: Most people do.

NARRATOR: Each day, the seven vertically challenged persons went to work at their advertising and PR company, whistling a merry tune as they did so. (*He whistles 'Whistle while you work ... '*)

MINISTRY MAN 1: (*Rings bell and looks serious*) Where did they get that tune?

NARRATOR: What do you mean?

MINISTRY MAN 2: They didn't down-load it from the Internet, did they?

MINISTRY MAN 1: Without paying?

MINISTRY MAN 2: Are you aware of the stringent copyright laws protecting music nowadays?

NARRATOR: Well, yes, but ...

MINISTRY MAN 1: The Disney Corporation comes down on any transgressors like a tonne of bricks.

MINISTRY MAN 2: That's tonne, t-o-n-n-e, since we've gone metric.

MINISTRY MAN 1: Quite.

NARRATOR: What do you suggest they whistle, then?

(*Ministry Man 1 and Ministry Man 2 confer.*)

MINISTRY MAN 1: Beethoven is out of copyright. How about a bit from the Pastoral Symphony? Oh, mind you, Olive Brown and the seven vertically challenged persons don't live in a wood now, do they? Better stick to the Eroica.

(*Narrator whistles snatch from Beethoven's Eroica Symphony.*)

MINISTRY MAN 2: (*To Ministry Man 1*) Always loved that …

NARRATOR: But one day, while they were at work in the advertising and PR company, Olive Brown was walking around the housing estate and she bumped into …

MINISTRY MAN 1: Now be very careful …

NARRATOR: … the Queen, disguised as a witch.

MINISTRY MAN 1: (*Shrugging*) Her private life's her own.

NARRATOR: The Queen gave her an apple to eat.

MINISTRY MAN 1: (*Rings bell*) Shrink-wrapped?

NARRATOR: Yes!

MINISTRY MAN 1: Fine.

NARRATOR: But when Olive Brown bit into it, she discovered that the apple was poisoned.

MINISTRY MAN 2: (*Suddenly seeing red and coming out as an ardent monarchist*) This is just too much! The Royal Family have got enough to worry about without being accused of poisoning food on housing estates. They get blamed for everything. The poor old Queen …

MINISTRY MAN 1: Ahem …

MINISTRY MAN 2: The relatively well-off and of-advancing-years Queen. I mean she only costs up 61p each a year. What could be better value for money? She's got problems with her children, she's got all those houses to look after in London and Norfolk and Scotland – where would she find the time to wander around

housing estates poisoning apples to bump off Olive
Brown? She's probably never even heard of her.

MINISTRY MAN 1: (*Pacifying him*) There, there. I know. But
you musn't let your personal feelings affect your job.

MINISTRY MAN 2: (*Opening his heart*) I know, but some
days you just get, well, you know, fed up with it all.

NARRATOR: (*Trying to be helpful*) Would it help if I told a
different story?

MINISTRY MAN 1: It might do. I'm sorry. He just gets a bit
overwrought from time to time. It's a difficult job,
treading a fine line. Sometimes the strain's too much.

MINISTRY MAN 2: (*Blowing his nose in a hanky*) I'll be fine
now. Sorry about that. (*To Ministry Man 1*) At least we
didn't have to worry about sex, drink and drugs.

NARRATOR: (*Rummaging through book*) I've found a
different one.

MINISTRY MAN 1: (*To Ministry Man 2*) He's found a
different one. You'll be all right now.

NARRATOR: This is the tale of Cinderella.

MINISTRY MAN 1: What's that all about?

NARRATOR: It's about a fit bit of totty who ditches her
ugly sisters and her mean old dad, goes to an all-night
rave where she gets absolutely slaughtered, then bonks
a prince senseless and lives happily ever after.

(*Ministry Man 2 runs from stage sobbing hysterically,
chased by Ministry Man 1.*)

THE END

# Family and Friends

*Christmas is a time for reacquainting yourself with your family – all those relations who are perfectly capable of cooking their own meals for the rest of the year, but who are happy to eat you out of house and home come December. But it will be fun. Won't it?*

## WHAT DO I WISH YOU?
*Charlotte Gray*

The family reunited,
All squabbles set aside,
Food in the larder,
Knocks at the door,
Friendly faces,
Parcels piling up,
Cards from everyone you love,
Nothing forgotten,
Nothing singed,
Laughter, a little silliness,
Hugs, kisses,
Happy memories.
I wish with all my heart that
your Christmas will be all that it
was meant to be –
a little warmth in the depth of
winter, a light in the dark.

## from THE PICKWICK PAPERS
*Charles Dickens*

Now the screaming had subsided, and faces were in a glow and curls in a tangle, and Mr. Pickwick, after kissing the old lady as before-mentioned, was standing under the mistletoe, looking with a very pleased countenance on all that was passing around him, when the young lady with the black eyes, after a little whispering with the other young ladies, made a sudden dart forward, and, putting her arm round Mr. Pickwick's neck, saluted him affectionately on the left cheek; and before Mr. Pickwick distinctly knew what was the matter, he was surrounded by the whole body, and kissed by every one of them.

It was a pleasant thing to see Mr. Pickwick in the centre of the group, now pulled this way, and then that, and first kissed on the chin and then on the nose, and then on the spectacles, and to hear the peals of laughter which were raised on every side; but it was a still more pleasant thing to see Mr. Pickwick, blinded shortly afterwards, with a silk-handkerchief, falling up against the wall, and scrambling into corners, and going through all the mysteries of blind-man's buff, with the utmost relish for the game, until at last he caught one of the poor relations; and then had to evade the blind man himself, which he did with a nimbleness and agility that elicited the admiration and applause of all beholders. The poor relations caught just the people whom they thought would like it; and when the game flagged, got caught themselves. When they were all tired of blind-man's buff, there was a great game at snap-dragon, and when fingers enough were burned with that, and all the raisins gone, they sat down by the huge fire of blazing logs to a substantial supper, and a mighty bowl of wassail, something smaller than an ordinary washhouse copper, in which the hot apples were hissing and bubbling with a rich look, and a jolly sound, that were perfectly irresistible.

'This,' said Mr. Pickwick, looking round him, 'this is, indeed, comfort.'

*Well, it'll happen one way or the other. Either you'll have to go to them or they'll have to come to you. The only way round it is to go on a cruise. Still, it might turn out to be more fun than you think. Unless you're Adrian Mole …*

From THE GROWING PAINS OF
ADRIAN MOLE
*Sue Townsend*

I was glad when Auntie Susan and her friend Gloria turned up; at 11 o'clock. Their talk is very metropolitan and daring; and Gloria is dead glamorous and sexy. She wears frilly dresses, and lacy tights, and high heels. And she's got an itsy-bitsy voice that makes my stomach go soft. Why she's friends with Auntie Susan, who is a prison warder, smokes Panama cigars and has got hairy fingers, I'll never know.

The turkey was OK. But would have been better if the giblets and the plastic bag had been removed before cooking. Bert made chauvinist remarks during the carving. He leered at Gloria's cleavage and said, 'Give me a nice piece of breast.' Gloria wasn't a bit shocked, but I went dead red, and pretended that I'd dropped my cracker under the table.

When my mother asked me which part of the turkey I wanted, I said, 'A wing please!' I really wanted breast, leg, or thigh. But wing was the only part of the bird without sexual connotations. Rosie had a few spoons of

125

mashed potato and gravy. Her table manners are disgusting, even worse than Bert's.

I was given a glass of Bull's Blood wine and felt dead sensual. I talked brilliantly and with consummate wit for an hour, but then my mother told me to leave the table, saying, 'One sniff of the barmaid's apron and his mouth runs away with him.'

The Queen didn't look very happy when she was giving her speech. Perhaps she got lousy Christmas presents this year, like me. Bert and Auntie Susan had a disagreement about the Royal Family. Bert said he would 'move the whole lot of 'em into council houses in Liverpool.'

Gloria said, 'Oh Bert that's a bit drastic. Milton Keynes would be more suitable. They're not used to roughing it you know.'

In the evening I went round to see Grandma and my father. Grandma forced me to eat four mincepies, and asked me why I wasn't wearing my new Balaclava helmet. My father didn't say anything; he was dead drunk in an armchair.

*from* THE DIARY OF A NOBODY
*George and Weedon Grossmith*

CHRISTMAS DAY. We caught the 10.20 train at Paddington, and spent a pleasant day at Carrie's [his wife's] mother's. The country was quite nice and pleasant, although the roads were sloppy. We dined in the middle of the day, just ten of us, and talked over old times. If everybody had a nice, *un*interfering mother-in-law, such as I have, what a deal of happiness there would be in the world. Being all in good spirits, I proposed her health; and I made, I think, a very good speech.

I concluded, rather neatly, by saying: 'On an occasion like this – whether relatives, friends, or acquaintances – we are all inspired with good feelings towards each other. We are of one mind, and think only of love and friendship. Those who have quarrelled with absent friends should kiss and make up. Those who happily have *not* fallen out can kiss all the same.'

I saw the tears in the eyes of both Carrie and her mother, and must say I felt very flattered by the compliment. That dear old Reverend John Panzy Smith, who married us, made a most cheerful and amusing speech, and said he should act on my suggestion respecting the kissing. He then walked round the table and kissed all the ladies, including Carrie. Of course one did not object to this: but I was more than staggered when a young fellow named Moss, who was a stranger to me, and who had scarcely spoken a word through dinner, jumped up suddenly with a sprig of mistletoe, and exclaimed: 'Hulloh! I don't see why I shouldn't be in on this scene.' Before one could realize what he was about to do, he kissed Carrie and the rest of the ladies.

Fortunately the matter was treated as a joke, and we all laughed; but it was a dangerous experiment, and I felt very uneasy for a moment as to the result. I subsequently referred to the matter to Carrie, but she said: 'Oh, he's not much more than a boy.' I said that he had a very large moustache for a boy. Carrie replied: 'I didn't say he was not a nice boy.'

DECEMBER 26. I did not sleep very well last night; I never do in a strange bed. I feel a little indigestion, which one must expect at this time of the year. Carrie and I returned to Town in the evening. Lupin came in late. He said he enjoyed his Christmas, and added: 'I feel as fit as a Lowther Arcade fiddle, and only require a little more "oof" to feel as fit as a £500 Stradivarius.' I have long since given up trying to understand Lupin's slang, or asking him to explain it.

*At least nowadays we can all sit round the telly, instead of having to talk to one another. Imagine what it must have been like in the days when you could do nothing but make polite conversation …*

*from* THE DIARY OF A PROVINCIAL LADY
*E.M. Delafield*

*December 24th.* – Take entire family to children's party at neighbouring Rectory. Robin says Damn three times in the Rector's hearing, an expression never used by him before or since, but apparently reserved for this unsuitable occasion. Party otherwise highly successful, except that I again meet recent arrival at the Grange, on whom I have not yet called. She is a Mrs. Somers, and is said to keep Bees. Find myself next to her at tea, but cannot think of anything to say about Bees, except Does she *like* them, which sounds like a bad riddle, so leave it unsaid and talk about Preparatory Schools instead. (Am interested to note that no two parents ever seem to have heard of one another's Preparatory Schools. Query: Can this indicate an undue number of these establishments throughout the country?)

After dinner, get presents ready for children's stockings. William unfortunately steps on small glass article of doll's furniture intended for Vicky, but handsomely offers a shilling in compensation, which I refuse. Much time taken up in discussing this. At eleven p.m. children still wide awake. Angela suggests Bridge and asks Who is that Mrs. Somers we met at the Rectory, who seems to be interested in Bees? (A. evidently more skilled than myself in social amenities, but do not make this comment aloud.)

*Xmas Day.–* Festive, but exhausting Christmas. Robin and Vicky delighted with everything, and spend much of the day eating. Vicky presents her Aunt Angela with small square of canvas on which blue donkey is worked in cross-stitch. Do not know whether to apologise for this or not, but eventually decide better to say nothing, and hint to Mademoiselle that other design might have been preferable.

The children perhaps rather too much *en évidence*, as Angela, towards tea-time, begins to tell me that the little Maitlands have such a delightful nursery, and always spend entire day in it except when out for long walks with governess and dogs.

William asks if that Mrs. Somers is one of the Dorsetshire lot – a woman who knows about Bees. Make a note that I really must call on Mrs. S. early next week. Read up something about Bees before going.

Turkey and plum-pudding cold in the evening, to give the servants a rest. Angela looks at bulbs, and says What made me think they would be in flower for Christmas? Do not reply to this, but suggest early bed for us all.

# CHRISTMAS DAY, 1955
*Noel Coward*

Beverley Hills

In the middle of it all again. This house is really very nice and I have a dusky Jamaican lady to look after me who is lackadaisical and hums constantly. There have been a series of parties as usual, each one indistinguishable from the other, culminating last night in the [Humphrey] Bogarts' Christmas Eve revel which was great fun and highly glamorous to the eye. The Christmas shopping has been frantic as usual. Clifton [Webb] is sweet but inclined to bouts of slightly bibulous self-pity on account of being lonely. Mabelle [Clifton's mother] is indestructible and gets on his nerves, also he has no picture settled, so he is idle. We had a successful reading of the play at the Bogarts' last Sunday and everyone read well. Betty [Lauren] Bacall will be good, I think, and anyhow she is word perfect which is wonderful considering she was shooting a picture until yesterday.

I have acquired some nice Christmas loot. Exquisite gold and ebony monogrammed links from Frank Sinatra, and a lovely black dressing-gown and pyjamas to match from Marlene [Dietrich] and hand-worked bedroom slippers from Merle [Oberon] which are charming. A lot of other nice gifts too, but oh I *do* wish Christmas hadn't coincided with *Blithe Spirit*. There is so much to be done and, it seems, so little time to do it.

# Pride and Prunejuice

## A PLAY IN ONE ACT

*By Alan Titchmarsh*

*After Jane Austen (200 years after Jane Austen)*

---

*The parts of Mr Bennet, Lady Catherine and Mr Bingley are played by one male actor with fast costume changes, as are the parts of Mrs Bennet and Mr Collins, and Mr Darcy and Mr Wickham. Jane and Lydia are played by the same actress. The words 'actor' and 'actress' are used loosely. Carl Davis's music for* Pride and Prejudice *is the perfect accompaniment on the pianoforte.*

CHARACTERS

NARRATOR – upright and authoritative
MR BENNET – the bored father
MRS BENNET – the hysterical mother
JANE – beautiful
LIZZIE – sensible and feisty
LYDIA – no better than she should be
MARY – at the piano (preferably a camp man
in a bonnet)
LADY CATHERINE DE BOURGH – Dame Edith Evans
MR COLLINS – an oily and obsequious cleric
MR DARCY – hunk with rod up back
MR BINGLEY – nice chap
MR WICKHAM – dastardly bounder

LIZZIE: It is a truth universally acknowledged that a single man in possession of a good fortune, must be in want of a wife.

NARRATOR: So wrote Jane Austen in the opening sentence of *Pride and Prejudice*. But one is forced to conjecture just how well the book would have done had she not been such a good writer.

MR DARCY: Badly.

NARRATOR: And I'm sure Mr Darcy spoke for us all.

MR WICKHAM: He usually does.

NARRATOR: And so we present *Pride and Prunejuice*, an everyday story of Georgian country folk.

(FX: *Music.*)

NARRATOR: The year is 1813. The county is Hampshire, and Sir Thomas Miller (*puts on costume*) is about to entertain his family by reading them the new story from Miss Jane Austen, whose previous novel, *Sense and Sensuality*, had been impounded by the censor just a couple of years before. We begin our story in the house of the Bennet family. As ever, Mr Bennet has his head stuck in a book. Usually something from the top shelf. Of his library. He is endeavouring to escape the incessant nagging of his wife.

(*Mr Bennet enters, head stuck in a book.*)

MRS BENNET: (*Hysterically chatty*) Oh Mr Bennet, I don't know what I'm going to do with you. Five daughters all unmarried and no earthly sign of them being otherwise and all you can do is stick your head in a book. Why do you do it, oh why do you do it?

MR BENNET: I'm sorry, I can't hear you. I have my head stuck in a book.

MRS BENNET: But why, Mr Bennet, why?

MR BENNET: I got rather too close to the glue, dear.

MRS BENNET: (*Pulls him off – he has half a ripped page stuck to his forehead*) Oh, Mr Bennet!

MR BENNET: Ow!

MRS BENNET: You really have no time for such idle pursuits now, Mr Bennet, not with Netherparts Hall being taken.

MR BENNET: Taken?

MRS BENNET: Yes, taken!

MR BENNET: Netherparts Hall?

MRS BENNET: Yes, taken by a young man – a single young man of large fortune – four or five thousand a year. What a fine thing for our girls!

MR BENNET: Is his sight quite good?

MRS BENNET: What *do* you mean, Mr Bennet?

MR BENNET: Can he see?

MRS BENNET: Perfectly well. Perfectly well.

MR BENNET: Then I fear he will have no interest in them. Now were you to tell me that he is a myopic millionaire with no taste and even less style, I would be inclined to be more hopeful on the marital front. As it is, I fear that not even my darling Lizzie will be able to captivate him.

MRS BENNET: But how can you say that, Mr Bennet? Are not my daughters beautiful and captivating? Would they not turn the head of the most exacting gentleman?

MR BENNET: They would.

MRS BENNET: Then why on earth do you say they will be unlikely to find a suitor?

MR BENNET: Because you are their mother.

MRS BENNET: (*Totally hysterical now*) Oh, Mr Bennet! How could you say such a thing? Am I not a model of motherhood? Have I not cherished my five daughters these twenty-three years and cared for them and tried to put them in the way of suitable men?

MR BENNET: (*Icy calm and slow*) Yes.

MRS BENNET: Then how can you say such a cold and hurtful thing? Cold and hurtful it is, Mr Bennet. Cold and hurtful. How can you say such a thing?

MR BENNET: Because it's true.

MRS BENNET: Oh, Mr Bennet! I shall never speak to you again, do you hear? Never, never, never!

(*She runs from the stage shrieking.*)

MR BENNET: You will.

NARRATOR: Mr and Mrs Bennet have, as you are now aware, five daughters. The elegant, serene Jane …

JANE: Elegant, elegant, serene, serene.

NARRATOR: The feisty Lizzie …

LIZZIE: Feist, feist.

NARRATOR: The bookish Mary, who plays the piano … (*Mary plays piano and looks engagingly at audience*) … Thank you, Mary, you have delighted us long enough … Kitty, who nobody can remember … (*watches invisible girl walk across stage*) … And Lydia, who was no better than she should be …

LYDIA: Phwoar!

NARRATOR: And now things will begin to hot up for the Misses Bennet, for besides Mr Bingley …

MR BINGLEY: … for some unaccountable reason named after a suburb of Bradford …

NARRATOR: … famous only as the headquarters of the

Sports Turf Research Institute … (*all cast look at him as though he's lost it*) – I only drop it in as a matter of interest … (*all cast yawn*)

MR BINGLEY: … but with quite a pleasant demeanour nevertheless …

NARRATOR: … there is also Mr Darcy.

ALL LADIES: Aaaaaaaaaah!

(*Darcy smoulders and broods.*)

NARRATOR: Mr Darcy owns Plumpily, a handsome estate in Derbyshire, and is a man of considerable pride who made his fortune from the sales of a natural laxative. Hence the title of Miss Austen's work, *Pride and Prunejuice*. Unbeknownst to the Bennet family, he is intimately acquainted with the wicked Mr Wickham, whose greatest claim to fame is that he looks good in uniform.

(*Wickham enters wearing terrible uniform.*)

NARRATOR: Usually. But there are two other flies in the ointment of life at Longbottom, the Bennet's modest country stool. (That's rather like a country seat but not quite so grand.) The first is …

LADY CATHERINE DE BOURGH: … Lady Catherine de Bourgh.

NARRATOR: Who, as you can see, is an aristocratic *grande dame* of hideous aspect, determined that the Bennet family will not get on in society, and equally determined that Elizabeth Bennet shall not enjoy any kind of society with Mr Darcy.

LIZZIE: Not even Operatic Society?

NARRATOR: No! The last of our characters, for we must, perforce, be brief …

LIZZIE: … unlike a BBC2 classic serial, which can take several weeks to reach its denouement …

NARRATOR: … is Mr Collins.

MR COLLINS: How simply wonderful to be mentioned in the same breath as Lady Catherine de Bourgh, and even to perambulate upon the same timbers that constitute this rude erection.

LADY CATHERINE: Mr Collins!

MR COLLINS: Lady Catherine!

NARRATOR: Mr Collins is a clergyman. A clergyman of oleaginous tendencies.

MR COLLINS: They can't touch me for it.

MARY: Ole-what?

NARRATOR: Oleaginous. It's actually derived from the Latin name of the olive – *Olea* – and it means oily. Funny, isn't it, how plants seem to creep into everything?

MARY: Hilarious.

NARRATOR: But back to our story. Mr Bingley's ball is to be held at Netherparts.

MARY: Ooh! Nasty!

NARRATOR: No, it will be a wonderful ball, and we shall see how our characters get on.

MARY: Get on his ball?

NARRATOR: No, get on *at* his ball! (I think you should have played Lydia.)

MR WICKHAM: I should have liked to have played *with* Lydia.

NARRATOR: You will, Oscar, you will.


(FX: *Music for the ball.*)


MR BINGLEY: Tell me, Miss Jane Bennet, for I must call you that in order to distinguish you from all your sisters who, in spite of there being five of you, seem to look like just two …

JANE: Yes, Mr Bingley?

MR BINGLEY: Do you come here often?

JANE: No; you've never invited me before.

MR BINGLEY: That would explain it.

JANE: Explain what?

MR BINGLEY: Why you dance so badly.

MR DARCY: Miss Elizabeth Bennet …

LIZZIE: Yes, Mr Darcy?

MR DARCY: Has anyone else ever remarked on your similarity to your sisters?

LIZZIE: Only Mr Bingley.

MR DARCY: That would explain it.

LIZZIE: Explain what?

MR DARCY: I don't know. I've rather lost the plot. If it's all the same to you, I think I'll just stand here and look aloof for a while.

LIZZIE: Is that wise? It looks like rain.

MR DARCY: That's all right. I have my wet shirt with me.

ALL GIRLS: Aaaaaah!

LADY CATHERINE: (*To narrator*) Young man!

NARRATOR: Yes?

LADY CATHERINE: I've had nothing to say for ages.

NARRATOR: No. But you will. You always do.

MR COLLINS: And you always do it so well, Lady Catherine, your tones are always so mellifluous, and your sentiments so generous in their magnanimity.

LADY CATHERINE: How terribly unctuous.

NARRATOR: But what of Lydia, the Bennet's youngest daughter, who has her sights set on the dashing Mr Wickham?

LYDIA: (*To Wickham*) Phwoar!

MR WICKHAM: I'm sorry?

LYDIA: Phwoar!

MR WICKHAM: I thought that's what you said. Do you fancy a bit round the back of the bike shed?

NARRATOR: But unfortunately, bike sheds had not yet caught on, so they had to settle for a barouche round the back of Bingley's ballroom.

LYDIA: Oh, Mr Wickham, that was some barouche!

MR WICKHAM: (*Wickedly*) I know.

NARRATOR: Meanwhile, Lizzie and Mr Darcy are not getting on too well …

MR DARCY: Your dancing is rather stiff, Miss Bennet.

LIZZIE: That's not the only thing that's stiff, Mr Darcy.

MR DARCY: I beg your pardon?

LIZZIE: Have you always had a problem with your hauteur?

MR DARCY: Only since I caught it in the back of Mr Bingley's barouche.

LIZZIE: Perhaps you should have it looked at.

MR DARCY: We are a very private family.

NARRATOR: And so Mr Darcy lost another chance to get closer to Elizabeth Bennet, all on account of his enormous hauteur.

LYDIA: Phwoar!

LIZZIE: It wasn't that big really. Not when you got close.

LYDIA: Oh. Shame.

NARRATOR: But what of Mr and Mrs Bennet while all this is going on?

MRS BENNET: Oh, Mr Bennet, look at Mr Darcy with our Lizzie and Mr Wickham with Lydia. Isn't he dashing?

MR BENNET: Not particularly.

MRS BENNET: I'm sure we shall have two sons-in-law by Michaelmas, Mr Bennet, and our troubles will be at an end.

MR BENNET: I wish.

MRS BENNET: Can you imagine, Mr Bennet, adding Netherparts and Plumpily to the Longbottom estate. What would that produce?

MR BENNET: Acute discomfort I should think.

MRS BENNET: (*Ignoring him*) Oh, Mr Bennet, what do you wish for more than anything else in the world?

MR BENNET: Deafness.

NARRATOR: Yes, things are pretty much as we left them with Mr and Mrs Bennet. But Mr Collins is making a move on Miss Elizabeth.

MR COLLINS: Miss Elizabeth Bennet, would you care for a quadrille?

LIZZIE: No thank you. I've already eaten.

MR COLLINS: A minuet then?

LIZZIE: Oh, very well, if I must.

MR COLLINS: That is so kind of you, Miss Elizabeth. (*Very rapidly*) I have been admiring you these past months, and I must confess that I have been singularly drawn to you. Your movement, your carriage, your coquettish attitude to me. Tell me it is not my imagination, Miss Bennet. Tell me that these are not the ramblings of a poor, wandering soul who is destined to remain earthbound while the spirit of his inamorata soars, swallow-like, into the cerulean blue yonder of his imagination. Tell your poor suitor that his ardour is not spent in futile pursuit of the unattainable; that he is not casting his pearls before the swine of contempt in a pitilessly pointless entreaty that may yet result in his being cast unceremoniously into emotional oblivion on account of the unreciprocated pleadings that fall, redundant, on the aural orifices of the sole object of his affections.

LIZZIE: No.

MR COLLINS: Oh.

NARRATOR: And is Mr Wickham having any better fortune with Lydia?

LYDIA: Phwoar!

MR WICKHAM: All right, darlin'?

LYDIA: Phwoar!

NARRATOR: Alas, Miss Lydia Bennet is, to use a

contemporary expression, 'no better than she should be'. But she may improve. While her sisters add skills such as needlepoint and silhouette painting to their repertoire, Lydia is already perfecting a new accomplishment.

*(Lydia whistles at Wickham.)*

NARRATOR: Alas, the new skill is unlikely to endear itself to Mr Darcy, who has been oblivious to high-pitched noises since birth.

MR DARCY: I have been oblivious to high-pitched noises since birth.

NARRATOR: I've just said that.

MR DARCY: I thought I'd reiterate.

LYDIA: I love it when you reiterate.

DARCY: Thank you.

NARRATOR: But the quieter of the Bennet sisters, Kitty, has been dancing all evening.

*(Music plays and the cast watch the invisible Kitty dance across the floor.)*

LIZZIE: She never says much.

NARRATOR: And Mary has been playing the piano. (*Mary plays the piano.*) She's never happier than when she can get her hands on an old upright. And if it's a grand, she's even happier. Oh, the countless jolly times the Bennets have had watching Mary run her fingers over the vicar's organ of a Sunday, with a twinkle in her eye and colour in her cheeks. Even the vicar himself says that when it comes to scales and arpeggios, no one handles his instrument quite like Mary. But what's this? Mr Bingley is making a move on Miss Jane Bennet.

MR BINGLEY: Miss Jane Bennet! I have got the right one, haven't I?

JANE: I don't know. I haven't looked.

MR BINGLEY: Miss Bennet, I know I have been a little lax …

JANE: There are tablets, Mr Bingley.

MR BINGLEY: I know I have been a little lax in my affections.

JANE: There's ointment for that.

MR BINGLEY: Hear me out, I entreat you. Make me a happy man!

JANE: But how could I do that?

MR BINGLEY: Introduce me to your mother.

NARRATOR: It is a cruel twist of the plot! Miss Jane Bennet, usually serene and elegant …

JANE: Serene, serene, elegant, elegant.

NARRATOR: … is now distraught with grief and recrimination.

JANE: Grief, grief, rec … rec … grief.

NARRATOR: And Mr Darcy is approaching Mr Bennet. Why could that be?

MR DARCY: Mr Bennet.

MR BENNET: Mr Darcy.

MR DARCY: I have to tell you that for some time I have been watching your every move.

MR BENNET: Really?

MR DARCY: And there have been very few of them.

MR BENNET: Does it show?

MR DARCY: Little escapes my trained eye.

MR BENNET: Ah. I see.

MR DARCY: Have you considered prune juice?

MR BENNET: Would it help?

MR DARCY: It usually does.

MR BENNET: Then I shall try it. Dash it! Yes, I shall try it.

MR DARCY: You will not regret it, Mr Bennet.

MRS BENNET: We must make a move, Mr Bennet.

MR BENNET: I think I shall, dear.

MR DARCY: Within the hour, Mr Bennet.

MR BENNET: So soon?

MR DARCY: Maybe sooner.

MR BENNET: Then we must go.

NARRATOR: But Mr Bingley is determined to meet Mrs Bennet, and while Mr Bennet dashes for the nearest exit, he interrupts her society with Mr Darcy.

MR BINGLEY: Mrs Bennet.

MRS BENNET: Yes?

MR BINGLEY: Don't deny it!

MRS BENNET: No.

MR BINGLEY: I must have intercourse with you.

MRS BENNET: Then come over to the banquette.

MR BENNET: Won't that be rather uncomfortable?

MRS BENNET: It's overstuffed.

MR BENNET: Well, it is Christmas.

MRS BENNET: Quite.

MR BENNET: I have to ask you something covertly.

MRS BENNET: Don't call me covertly.

MR BENNET: Very well. I must ask you something in confidence.

MRS BENNET: Couldn't you ask me in Winchester?

LYDIA: Phwoar!

NARRATOR: What?

LYDIA: I haven't 'Phwoar'd' for a bit, that's all.

NARRATOR: Meanwhile, Mr Darcy is approaching Lady Catherine De Bourgh.

MR BINGLEY: Hang on a minute. (*Puts bonnet on*)

NARRATOR: He has been running his eye over Miss Elizabeth Bennet and has decided to make his overtures to Lady Catherine. (*Mary plays the start of an overture.*) Not that sort of overture. (*Mary starts another overture.*) Or that one. No, he wants to sound Lady Catherine out over a possible liaison. (*Lady Catherine comes on stage, panting but ready.*) But he changes his mind and decides instead to warn his friend Mr Bingley that something's afoot. (*Lady Catherine changes again into Bingley*)

MR BINGLEY: What's afoot?

MR DARCY: That funny thing on the end of your leg.

MR BINGLEY: (*To narrator*) Did you make me change just for that?

NARRATOR: Seemed like a good idea at the time. But Mr Bennet is approaching …

MR BINGLEY: Oh, give us a break!

NARRATOR: They didn't say that in Georgian times.

MR BINGLEY: Don't you mean Gregorian?

*(Mary sings Gregorian chant.)*

NARRATOR: No. But I think it's time we got to the bottom of this plot.

LIZZIE: Longbottom?

NARRATOR: Not from where I'm standing.

MR BINGLEY: Netherparts?

NARRATOR: Those as well.

MR DARCY: *(Irritably)* Miss Bennet?

LYDIA: Which one?

MR DARCY: The other one.

LYDIA: Oh.

MR DARCY: Will you marry me?

LIZZIE: Only if you wear a wet shirt.

*(Narrator squirts Darcy with hand-mister.)*

MR DARCY: Will you marry me?

LIZZIE: Well, you are a bit wet, but yes.

MR DARCY: My own!

LIZZIE: My love!

LYDIA: What about me? Where's my Wickham?

NARRATOR: Just south of Amersham.

LYDIA: *(Sarcastically)* That's *High* Wycombe.

*(Mr Darcy throws on army jacket and moustache.)*

MR WICKHAM: Here I am my love!

LYDIA: I didn't recognize you for a moment.

MARY: (*At piano – to audience*) I'm sorry. I mean this really is drivel, isn't it? What is the point? You take a perfectly decent book and you reduce it to this travesty.

NARRATOR: Thank you, Mary. And how long have you had this problem?

MARY: (*Emotionally*) Several weeks now. It's just got worse and worse.

LADY CATHERINE: Then it's time you were relieved. Roughage, dear. That's what you need. Roughage.

MR DARCY: And there's no finer way of getting it than this: Darcy's Patent Prunejuice.

MARY: But will it really work?

MR DARCY: Oh yes. I take pride in my prunejuice. Two tablespoonfuls at mealtimes and you'll soon notice the difference.

NARRATOR: And Mary did. Within no time at all her movements were back to normal. (*Mary plays several bars of elaborate music.*) And so it was that the Bennet family married off all their daughters, and Miss Jane Austen went on to write more novels, but all of them owed much to the success of *Pride and Prunejuice*. None more so than the one named in its honour after her eponymous heroine. It was subsequently entitled 'Emma' but we know that originally it was going to be called …

ALL: … ENEMA!


CURTAIN

# The Nativity

*At the heart of Christmas is the greatest story ever told –
of Mary and Joseph, and of the baby Jesus born in the
stable. Most of us were brought up on the nativity –*
Away in a Manger *was probably the first carol we sang as
children – and it remains a magical story. Each year, in
December, the story is recounted in primary schools across
the land, with small boys as shepherds wearing tea towels
on their heads, and old velvet curtains called into service
for the kings. Of course, it's just a story. It couldn't
happen today, could it?*

# A NEW NATIVITY
*Alan Titchmarsh*

When all those long, long years ago
A child came down to earth below,
To save the likes of you and me
From evil, harm and misery

Do you suppose that even then
There were some doubting, heedless men
Who rather than believe the word
Just turned their backs and never heard?

You see, today we all recall
The baby in the ox's stall
The ass, the stables, shepherds, Kings,
All ancient, rural, rustic things.

But what if here, this very night,
It happened … on the Isle of Wight.
Would we rejoice and all be merry?
Would we dash off and catch the ferry?

If Christ was born in Walthamstow,
Would builders drop their tools and go?
Would Wapping printers stop their presses?
Would supermodels ditch their dresses?

In Hampshire and in rural Kent,
Would shepherds by an angel sent
Walk miles to see a newborn child,
Whose mother, unmarried, although mild,

Had given birth to a baby boy,
Not at the Dorchester or Savoy,
But in a garage, there's the rub,
Round the back of the local pub.

The boy's dad hadn't been to college,
And of the child he claims no knowledge;
Saying that an angel came
To tell his wife the baby's name.

Just a joiner; nothing grand,
No previous form, their records scanned,
The police confirmed when sent to see,
The saviour of humanity.

If Jesus Christ was born today
In newspapers instead of hay,
I doubt He'd even come to be
In *News at Ten*'s 'and finally'.

For now it's hard to be impressed
With goodness, gentleness and blessed
With something more than mere sensation,
A baby, born to save a nation?

'Some tearaway; two homeless louts'
The newspaper proprietor shouts;
'Just print the story, headlines large:
Christmas Baby Born In Garage.'

No shepherds, no kings, no golden parcel;
No prince from inside Windsor Castle
Following the star with brightest glow,
To the garage behind the pub in Walthamstow.

And yet I like to think that we,
Despite the e-mail and DVD,
Would know to go, when star shone bright
And make that journey through the night.

To see the child who saves the world,
In some old oil drum safely curled;
The nativity for the millennium.
Would anyone out there like to come?

*This is a personal book, so I can allow myself the odd indulgence. My eldest daughter Polly wrote this at primary school when she was six. I still have the original written in soft pencil and decorated with coloured crayons. Her spelling has improved; so has her punctuation. She's a teacher now.*

## MARY AND THE BABBY

Once upon a time there was a lady was called mery and she was going to have a babby but the fery told her that and it was trau thay rid on a donky up in Bethleyhem they stayd in a stabull and they had the babby in the stabull they lid him a bit of stroy with a pes of caton on his tomey.

*Hollie Simpson was a pupil at the same school a few years later. This is her offering, given to me by her teacher. She's probably a university professor now. Or a Booker prize-winner.*

## A CHRISTMAS STORY
*Hollie Simpson* (age 6 years)

Once upon a time there was a little lady called Mary. She was cleaning her house. Suddenly an angel appeared. She was frightened.

The angel said: 'Don't be frightened. I only came to tell you that you will be having a baby king.'

'Wow,' said Mary.

'Bye,' said the angel, and the angel vanished.

Mary *was* pleased. Then Mary went to tell Joseph.

When she got there she said:

'Hey Joseph, guess what – I'm going to have a baby king.' Joseph was excited – they cuddled and Mary and Joseph had a little dance and then they heard some clip-clop-clip.

Then a messenger came along and said 'You have to go to where you were born.' So then they got a donkey and Joseph put Mary on and they set off with Joseph holding a lead and suddenly Mary said 'Oh, how far?', and Joseph saw a sign saying 77 miles. When Joseph said '77 miles' Mary almost fainted, but when they were able to see the sign saying 'Bethlehem' it was still a *long, long, long* way.

Then they reached Bethlehem.

It was crowded because there were all the people who lived there *and* the people who were born there. So when it was time to go to bed they went to an inn, and when the *first* innkeeper said 'It's full, sorry', the *second* innkeeper said 'Sorry, no room', and Joseph persuaded them. He kept saying 'I'm very worried about my wife – she will be having a baby.'

When they came to the *third* innkeeper he said 'Too late, full up, but you can stay in my stable,' so they did.

In the middle of the night Mary had a dreadful tummy ache and she had to lie down, and have 50 winks, and then she woke and she started to moan, then she had her baby.

Then some angels went up on hills and told some

shepherds up there and this is what they said:

'You go to Bethlehem to a lowly stable. There you will find a baby King.' So they did. They set off, only 3 of the shepherds took a sheep; 2 did not. When the shepherds got there they were amazed because they would not expect to find a baby king that's new in a stable.

Then the shepherds put the sheep down.

Then some Kings saw a star and they followed it. When they saw the stable they were feeling stupid because they thought the star should not be over a stable. So they opened the latch and they were amazed because they saw a baby and Mary and Joseph and some shepherds.

So they went in and gave a golden thing and a bit of frankincense that smells sweet and some myrrh for the pain when his teeth come through.

Then they celebrated for a bit of the night and all day until they had to be taxed.


## THE SECOND COMING …
*Alan Titchmarsh*

A friend of mine tells me of the time that she went to her small son's nativity play at the local primary school one afternoon in the week leading up to Christmas. There had been much in the way of preparations. Costumes had been cobbled together, all the angels had been found wings and the customary dolly had been wrapped in swaddling clothes. Emotions were running high.

When the great day arrived, the parents sat down in the audience to watch the performance. All went well until Mary and Joseph arrived at the inn and Joseph knocked at the door.

It was opened by the innkeeper.

'May we come in?' asked Joseph.

'No!' replied the innkeeper abruptly, and closed the door in their faces.

The little boy playing Joseph looked around him, nervously, then knocked again.

The innkeeper opened the door once more, and glowered at Joseph. 'What is it?'

'I am Joseph and this is my wife Mary. She is expecting a baby. May we come in?'

The innkeeper shook his head vigorously. 'No! You can't!' The door was slammed again. Joseph was getting more alarmed now, and banged on the door until the scenery shook. As the door was opened he asked, pleadingly:

'If there is no room in the inn, perhaps we could stay in your stable?'

'No. You can't!'

'But why?'

'Because I wanted to play Joseph.'

*Animals have their own part to play in the Christmas story – both those directly involved in the nativity and their descendants. Ursula Fanthorpe's poem is especially touching, and Thomas Hardy's* The Oxen *is an old favourite. Like him, I hope that it might be so.*

## WHAT THE DONKEY SAW
*U.A. Fanthorpe*

No room in the inn, of course,
And not that much in the stable,
What with the shepherds, Magi, Mary,
Joseph, the heavenly host –
Not to mention the baby
Using our manger as a cot.
You couldn't have squeezed another cherub in
For love or money.

Still, in spite of the overcrowding,
I did my best to make them feel wanted.
I could see the baby and I
Would be going places together.

# THE OXEN
*Thomas Hardy*

Christmas Eve, and twelve of the clock.
'Now they are all on their knees,'
An elder said as we sat in a flock
By the embers in hearthside ease.

We pictured the meek mild creatures where
They dwelt in their strawy pen,
Nor did it occur to one of us there
To doubt they were kneeling then.

So fair a fancy few would weave
In these years! Yet, I feel,
If someone said on Christmas Eve,
Come; see the oxen kneel,

'In the lonely barton by yonder coomb
Our childhood used to know,'
I should go with him in the gloom,
Hoping it might be so.

# CLASS DISTINCTION
*Alan Titchmarsh*

Class distinction. Nothing new;
Happened in Bethlehem
Out of the blue.

Animals have it. Rabbit, fox.
And in Bethlehem,
The ass, the ox.

But they rubbed along. Shared the straw.
And on that night
When the wind was raw

They'd settled down. Chewed the cud.
Scent of hay.
Dampness of mud.

The ox was dozing. The ass asleep.
Even the chickens
Slumbered deep;

Head under wing and feathers fluffed,
Hoping tomorrow
They wouldn't be stuffed.

All was quiet; then the door thrown wide,
And the innkeeper
Showed a young couple inside.

The ox and the ass didn't want to be moved,
But they stood up
As if they not only approved

But had waited for years for this star in the sky,
For the couple to come,
For the baby to cry.

They stood and they gazed in rapt delight
At the newborn child
In the golden light.

Then the door once more was flung open wide
And three kings walked in
Well, not so much a walk, more a glide.

They knelt by the babe and offered him gold,
And frankincense, myrrh,
A perfume of old.

The ox and the ass were just settling down,
When in strode a camel
In a golden gown.

From his fine gilded saddle hung tassels and braid;
His bridle bejewelled.
His demeanour displayed

A haughty indifference to all that he saw
And the ox and the ass
Although down on the floor

Took umbrage at the camel's profound disbelief,
And looked into his eyes
As he said 'Oh! Good grief!'

His lashes so long and his lip fully curled
He said 'Here? In a stable?
The King of the World?'

The ox and the ass, although never devoted,
Looked at each other
Then with their feet, voted.

Padding up to the camel, their shoulders set wide,
They nudged and they pushed
Till he landed outside.

'Look here!' he exclaimed, but they heard him not;
Just walked back inside
To the baby's cot.

They smiled at the infant of rosy hue;
Let out a bray,
Let out a moo.

The camel, indignant, by the bright star lit,
Thrashed his tail
And gave a spit.

From that day on, right up to now,
Men have muttered
'Holy cow!'

The ass, a cross upon his back,
Is much revered
And known as 'Jack'.

The camel, although grand and sneering,
Will never hear
The people cheering.

Because he thought the inn a dump
We give *him* what we call
The hump.


A YORKSHIRE NATIVITY
*From* HEAD OVER HEELS IN THE DALES
*Gervase Phinn*


The highlight of the evening in the first nativity play of
the Christmas season had been the Annunciation. Mary, a
pretty little thing of about six or seven, had been busy
bustling about the stage, wiping and dusting, when the
Angel of the Lord had appeared stage right.

The heavenly spirit had been a tall, self-conscious boy
with a plain, pale face and sticking-out ears. He had been
dressed in a flowing white robe, large paper wings, and
sported a crooked tinsel halo.

Having wiped his nose on his sleeve, he had glanced
around suspiciously and had sidled up to Mary, as a
dodgy market trader might to see if you were interested

in buying something from 'under the counter'.

'Who are you?' Mary had asked sharply, putting down her duster and placing her hands on her hips. This had not been the quietly spoken, gentle-natured Mary I had been used to.

'I am the Angel Gabriel,' the boy had replied with a dead-pan expression and in a flat voice.

'Well, what do you want?'

'Are you Mary?'

'Yes.'

'I come with tidings of great joy.'

'What?'

'I've got some good news.'

'What is it?'

'You're having a baby.'

'I'm not.'

'You are.'

'Who says?'

'God, and He sent me to tell you.'

'Well, I don't know nothing about this.'

'And it will be a boy and He will become great and be called – er, um – ' The boy stalled for a moment. 'Ah – called Son of the Most High, the King of Kings. He will rule for ever and his reign will have no end.'

'What if it's a girl?'

'It won't be.'

'You don't know, it might be.'

'It won't, 'cos God knows about these things.'

'Oh.'

'And you must call it Jesus.'

'I don't like the name Jesus. Can I call him something else?'

'No.'

'What about Gavin?'

'No.' The angel had snapped. 'You have to call it Jesus. Otherwise you don't get it.'

'Alright then,' Mary had agreed.

'And look after it.'

'I don't know what I'm going to tell Joseph,' the little girl had said, putting on a worried expression and picking up her duster.

'Tell him it's God's.'

'OK,' Mary had said, smiling for the first time.

When the Angel of the Lord had departed, Joseph had entered. He had been a cheeky-faced little boy dressed in a brown woollen dressing-gown, thick blue socks and a multi-coloured towel over his head held in place by the inevitable elastic belt with snake clasp.

'Hello, Mary,' he had said cheerfully.

'Oh hello, Joseph,' Mary had replied.

'Have you had a good day?'

'Yes, pretty good,' she had told him, nodding theatrically.

'Have you anything to tell me?'

There had been a slight pause before she had replied. 'I am having a baby – oh, and it's not yours.'

The audience had laughed and clapped at this, leaving the two small children rather bewildered.

The highlight of the second Nativity play had been after the entrance of the Three Kings. Someone had really gone to town on the costumes for the little boys, who came in clutching their gifts tightly. They were resplendent in gold and silver outfits, topped by large bejewelled crowns that shone brilliantly under the stage lights.

'I am the King of the North,' said one little boy, kneeling before the manger and laying down a brightly wrapped box. 'I bring you gold.'

'I am the King of the South,' said the second, kneeling before the manger and laying down a large coloured jar. 'I bring you myrrh.'

'I am the King of the East,' said the third and smallest child, kneeling before the manger and laying down a silver bowl. 'And Frank sent this.'


## THE BARN
*Elizabeth Coatsworth*

'I am tired of this barn!' said the colt.
'And every day it snows.
Outside there's no grass any more
And icicles grow on my nose.
I am tired of hearing the cows
Breathing and talking together.
I am sick of these clucking hens.
I hate stables and winter weather!'

'Hush, little colt,' said the mare.
'And a story I will tell
Of a barn like this one of ours
And the wonders that there befell.
It was weather much like this,
And the beasts stood as we stand now
In the warm good dark of the barn –
A horse and an ass and a cow.'

'And sheep?' asked the colt. 'Yes, sheep,
And a pig and a goat and a hen.
All of the beasts of the barnyard,
The usual servants of men.
And into their midst came a lady
And she was cold as death,
But the animals leaned above her
And made her warm with their breath.

'There was her baby born
And laid to sleep in the hay,
While music flooded the rafters
And the barn was as light as day.
And angels and kings and shepherds
Came to worship the babe from afar,
But we looked at him first of all creatures
By the bright strange light of a star!'

*Shepherds are a rare breed – self-sufficient men who know the ways of the countryside. Heywood Broun's story makes the shepherds of the nativity come to life.*

## A SHEPHERD
*Heywood Broun*

The host of heaven and the angel of the Lord had filled the sky with radiance. Now, the glory of God was gone and the shepherds and the sheep stood under dim starlight. The men were shaken by the wonders they had seen and heard, and, like the animals, they huddled close.

'Let us now,' said the eldest one of the shepherds, 'go even unto Bethlehem and see this thing which has come to pass, which the Lord hath made known unto us.'

The City of David lay beyond a far, high hill, upon the crest of which there danced a star. The men made haste to be away, but as they broke out of the circle there was one called Amos who remained. He dug his crook into the turf and clung to it.

'Come,' cried the eldest of the shepherds, but Amos shook his head. They marvelled, and called out: 'It is true. It was an angel. You heard the tidings. A Saviour is born!'

'I heard,' said Amos. 'I will abide.'

The eldest walked back from the road to the little knoll on which Amos stood.

'You do not understand,' the old man told him. 'We have a sign from God. An angel has commanded us. We go to worship the Saviour, who is even now born in Bethlehem. God has made His will manifest.'

'It is not in my heart,' replied Amos.

And now the eldest of the shepherds was angry.

'With your eyes,' he cried out, 'you have seen the host of heaven in these dark hills. And you heard, for it was like the thunder when "Glory to God in the Highest" came ringing to us out of the night.'

And again Amos said, 'It is not in my heart.'

Another then broke in: 'Because the hills still stand and the sky has not fallen it is not enough for Amos. He must have something louder than the voice of God.'

Amos held more tightly to his crook and answered, 'I have need of a whisper.'

They laughed at him and said, 'What should this voice say in your ears?'

He was silent, and they pressed about him and shouted mockingly: 'Tell us now. What says the God of Amos, the little shepherd of a hundred sheep?'

Meekness fell away from him. He took his hands from off the crook and raised them high.

'I, too, am a God,' said Amos in a loud, strange voice, 'and to my hundred I am a savior.'

And when the din of the angry shepherds about him slackened Amos pointed to his hundred.

'See my flock,' he said. 'See the fright of them. The fear of the bright angel and of the voices is still upon them. God is busy in Bethlehem. He has no time for a hundred sheep. They are my sheep. I will abide.'

This the others did not take so much amiss, for they saw that there was a terror in all the flocks, and they, too, knew the ways of sheep. And before the shepherds went away on the road to Bethlehem toward the bright star each one talked to Amos and told him what he should do for the care of the several flocks. And yet one or two turned back a moment to taunt Amos before they reached the dip in the road which led to the City of David. It was said, 'We shall see new glories at the throne of God, and you, Amos – you will see sheep.'

Amos paid no heed, for he thought to himself, 'One shepherd the less will not matter at the throne of God.' Nor did he have time to be troubled that he was not to see the Child who was come to save the world. There was much to be done among the flocks, and Amos walked between the sheep and made under his tongue a clucking noise, which was a way he had, and to his hundred and to the others it was a sound finer and more friendly than the voice of the bright angel. Presently the animals ceased to tremble and began to graze as the sun came up over the hill where the star had been.

'For sheep,' said Amos to himself, 'the angels shine too much. A shepherd is better.'

With the morning the others came up the road from Bethlehem, and they told Amos of the manger and of the wise men who had mingled there with shepherds. And they described to him the gifts – gold, frankincense and myrrh. And when they were done they said, 'And did you see wonders here in the field with the sheep?'

Amos told them, 'Now my hundred are one hundred and one,' and he showed them a lamb which had been born just before the dawn.

'Was there for this a great voice out of heaven?' asked the eldest of the shepherds.

Amos shook his head and smiled, and there was in his face that which seemed to the shepherds a wonder even in a night of wonders.

'To my heart,' he said, 'there came a whisper.'

*Nicholas Allan's version of the Christmas story has an innkeeper who seems to be Bethlehem's Basil Fawlty.*

## JESUS' CHRISTMAS PARTY
*Nicholas Allan*

There was nothing
the innkeeper liked
more than a good
night's sleep.

But that night there was
a knock at the door.

'No room,' said the innkeeper.
'But we're tired and have travelled
through night and day.'

'There's only the stable round the back.
Here's two blankets. Sign the register.'
So they signed it: 'Mary and Joseph.'

Then he shut the door,
climbed the stairs,
got into bed,
and went to sleep.

But then, later, there was
another knock at the door.

'Excuse me. I wonder if
you could lend us
another, smaller blanket?'
'There. One smaller blanket,'
said the innkeeper.

Then he shut the door,
climbed the stairs,
got into bed,
and went to sleep.

But then a bright light
woke him up.

'That's *all* I need,'
said the innkeeper.

Then he shut the door,
climbed the stairs,
drew the curtains,
got into bed,
and went to sleep.

But then there was *another*
knock at the door.

'We are three shepherds.'
'Well, what's the matter? Lost your sheep?'
'We've come to see Mary and Joseph.'
'ROUND THE BACK,'

said the innkeeper.
Then he shut the door,
climbed the stairs,
got into bed,
and went to sleep.

But then there was yet
*another* knock at the door.

'We are three kings. We've come –'

'ROUND THE BACK!'

He slammed the door,
climbed the stairs,

got into bed,
and went to sleep.

But *then* a chorus of
singing woke him up.

## 'RIGHT – THAT DOES IT!'

So he got out of bed,
stomped down the stairs,
threw open the door,
went round the back,
stormed into the stable,
and was just about to speak when –
'Ssshh!' whispered everybody,
'you'll wake the baby!'

'BABY?' said the innkeeper.

'Yes, a baby has this night been born.'

'Oh?' said the innkeeper, looking
crossly into the manger.

And just at that moment, suddenly,
amazingly, his anger seemed to fly away.
'Oh,' said the innkeeper, 'isn't he *lovely*!'

In fact, he thought he was so special …

he woke up *all* the guests at the inn,
so that they could come and have a look at the baby too.

So no one got much sleep that night!

*My friend Robert Salter is a solicitor. Having studied
the events of the nativity, he reckons that Joseph most
certainly had a case against the travel agents with whom
he booked the trip. He advised the sending of this letter:*

## THE SECOND EPISTLE FROM
## JOSEPH TO THE CORINTHIANS
*Robert Salter*

Dear Corinthians,
I acknowledge safe receipt of your epistle, in response to
my epistle (commonly known, for reasons that escape

me, as the first epistle to the Corinthians) concerning the recent sojourn with my wife, Mary, in Bethlehem or, as your brochure puts it, 'the City of David'.

For a travel company of repute, both Mary and I find your explanations of the accommodation arrangements far from satisfactory. If we have to make the journey again – which I hope we do not in the light of what occurred once we were there – it will most certainly not be with Corinthians 18–30 Holidays.

I offer the following response to your explanations:

(1) I have looked again at your brochure. I do not agree that the description of the Inn includes the outhouses. The words 'travellers with cattle can expect the use of the stables' surely refers to the cattle, not the guests. You may say that there are many worse off than ourselves – unfortunately they all seem to have booked with your company.

(2) You will have to take it from me that Mary giving birth to the Son of God was totally unexpected, and I can assure you that had I known He was on the way I would have given you the opportunity of bringing in your PR people.

(3) I agree with your proposition that from every point of view the story has more appeal set as it is in a stable rather than in the twin-bedded room with halfboard that we had booked. I also agree that it was much more convenient for the angel to make his way across the yard and into the stable rather than going through the

residents' lounge. Of course, I accept that the presence of the entire heavenly host praising God along the corridor on the second floor of the Inn might have resulted in complaints from your other guests. But that does not address my main complaint. My wife, Mary, has little in common with shepherds. It was bad enough having to cope with livestock in the stable, but having to face a deputation of local sheep-farmers who claimed they were tired of abiding in their fields at night was not our idea of 'local colour'. Your decision to include them as an optional extra in next year's brochure does not impress us.

(4) I know you are denying you had anything to do with the couriers who arrived from the east bearing gifts, but I still maintain that I had seen one of them in your office when I booked the trip. I do not wish to appear ungrateful, but at a time when I was struggling with a newly born child, an exhausted wife, a group of fanatical shepherds, assorted livestock, an angel explaining that my son was the Everlasting Father, and the entire heavenly host, the arrival of three Corinthian Holiday representatives in fancy dress did little to help. And, by the way, they could have left something a little more practical.

Yours very truly, Joseph

# On Christmas Day

*The great day itself. A time for giving. A time for over-indulgence. But hopefully, also a time to remember the true meaning of Christmas.*

## ST LUKE'S GOSPEL

And there were in the same country shepherds abiding in the field, keeping watch over their flock by night. And, lo, the angel of the Lord came upon them, and the glory of the Lord shone round about them: and they were sore afraid. And the angel said unto them, Fear not: for, behold, I bring you good tidings of great joy, which shall be to all people. For unto you is born this day in the city of David a Saviour, which is Christ the Lord.

### A CHRISTMAS LITANY
*Alan Titchmarsh*

Baubles
Glitter
Turkey
Steam
Pitter-patter
Holly
Cream

Ribbons
Crackers

Ho-ho-ho!
(Cough-cough)
Hackers
Mistletoe

Puddings
Stockings
Candlelight
Friendly knockings
In the night

Fairies
Santa
Logs that hiss!
Auntie Ada's prickly kiss
Cards
And carols
Full of cheer
Wine
And barrels
Full of beer!

Presents
Laughter
Stars
Snow
Bethlehem
Long ago.

Mary
Joseph
Shepherds
Kings
Oxen
Leopards
(rhymes with shepherds)
Angels
Wings.

Heavenly singing
Cherubs
Hay
Bells are ringing
Christmas Day!

*They talk about weather in the country, quite a lot. But then they always have done. The following entry is from the journal of the Reverend Gilbert White, who lived a few miles away from us in the village of Selborne in Hampshire. It is dated January 28th in the year of Our Lord 1768.*

Frost comes in a-doors. Little shining particles of ice appear on the ceiling, cornice and walls of the great parlour; the vapour condensed on the plaster is frozen in spite of frequent fires in the chimney. I now set a charing dish of clear burnt charcoal in the room on the floor.

On this day at 9 o'clock in the evening, Captain Lindsey's hands were frozen, as he was returning from Captain Dumeresque's to Rotherfield. The gent suffered Great pain all night, and found his nails turned black in the morning.

Horses are still falling with their general disorder. It freezes under people's beds. Rugged, Siberian weather. The narrow lanes are full of snow in some places, which is driven into most romantic and grotesque shapes. The road wagons are obliged to stop, and the stage coaches are much embarassed.

I must not omit to tell you that during those two Siberian days, my parlour cat was so electric, that had a person stroked her and been properly insulated, the shock might have been given to a whole circle of people.

I trust you will not be disappointed to hear these particulars, and especially when I promise to say no more about the severities of the winter after I have finished this letter.

## CHRISTMAS DAY
*Roy Fuller*

Small girls on trikes
Bigger on bikes
Collars on tykes

Looking like cads
Patterned in plaids
Scarf-wearing dads

Chewing a choc
Mum in a frock
Watches the clock

Knocking in pans
Fetching of grans
Gathering of clans

Hissing from tins
Sherries and gins
Upping of chins

Corks making pops
'Just a few drops'
Watering of chops

All this odd joy
Tears at a broken toy
Just for the birth long ago of a boy

*For most of us it is a time for loving and giving. But not all.*

## REMEMBER THEM
*Pam Brown*

We open our presents, laugh together, sit down to eat. But beyond the window – out there in the darkness – are those for whom Christmas brings no respite. For them it is another day of loneliness, fear, imprisonment, hunger, sickness, homelessness, weariness and war.

To many, even a shabby bedsitter would be a splendid place – dry, warm, safe and large enough to house a family. To many our full larders, our clean water, our health, our peace of mind, our united families are things of which they can only dream. Some knew our world once – and have lost it, or been exiled from it, or had it taken from them. Some have never known anything but fear and poverty and loss. It is right to show our love for one another at Christmas – to share a meal, to exchange gifts, to be happy.

But I wish that we privileged few could hear the voices of all those beyond our windows.

If only now, at Christmas, we could bring them in, share our thoughts and hear their individual stories. For they are not statistics, international problems, drains on government resources.

They are individuals, each complex and unique.

Valuable. As we are.

*George and Martha Washington had rather more to eat for their Christmas dinner at Mount Vernon than most. How would you fancy working your way through this?*

## CHRISTMAS DINNER

An Onion Soup call'd the King's Soup
Oysters on the Half Shell
Grilled Salt Roe Herring
Boiled Rockfish

———————

Roast Beef and Yorkshire Pudding
Mutton Chops
Roast Suckling Pig
Roast Turkey with Chestnut Stuffing
Round of Cold Boiled Beef with Horse-radish Sauce
Cold Baked Virginia Ham

Lima Beans
Baked Acorn Squash
Baked Celery with Silvered Almonds
Hominy Pudding
Candied Sweet Potatoes
Cantaloupe Pickle
Spiced Peaches in Brandy
Spiced Cranberries

———————

| | |
|---|---|
| Mincemeat Pie | Snowballs |
| Apple Pie | Indian Pudding |
| Cherry Pie | Great Cake |
| Chess Tarts | Ice Cream |
| Plums in Wine Jelly | Plum-Pudding |
| Blancmange | Fruits • Nuts • Raisins |

———————

Port • Madeira

# THE CHRISTMAS GOOSE
## From A CHRISTMAS CAROL
*Charles Dickens*

Mrs Cratchit made the gravy (ready beforehand in a little saucepan) hissing hot; Master Peter mashed the potatoes with incredible vigour; Miss Belinda sweetened up the apple-sauce; Martha dusted the hot plates; Bob took Tiny Tim beside him in a tiny corner at the table; the two young Cratchits set chairs for everybody, not forgetting themselves, and mounting guard upon their posts, crammed spoons into their mouths, lest they should shriek for goose before their turn came to be helped. At last the dishes were set on, and grace was said. It was succeeded by a breathless pause, as Mrs Cratchit, looking slowly all along the carving-knife, prepared to plunge it in the breast; but when she did, and when the long expected gush of stuffing issued forth, one murmur of delight arose all round the board, and even Tiny Tim, excited by the two young Cratchits, beat on the table with the handle of his knife, and feebly cried Hurrah!

There never was such a goose. Bob said he didn't believe there ever was such a goose cooked … Eked out by the apple-sauce and mashed potatoes, it was a sufficient dinner for the whole family; indeed, as Mrs Cratchit said with great delight (surveying one small atom of a bone upon the dish), they hadn't ate it all at last! Yet every one had had enough, and the youngest Cratchits in particular, were steeped in sage and onion to the eyebrows!

## CHRISTMAS PUDDING
*Alan Titchmarsh*

To make a Christmas pudding you need patience
And lots of time
    *Chorus* And lots of time

The recipe is long and very ancient
With barley wine
    *Chorus* With barley wine

First, you take a basin and some muslin
To seal the top
    *Chorus* To seal the top

Once you start the mixing it is tiring
You never stop
    *Chorus* You never stop

Grapes, sultanas, half a pound of plums,
Chopped bananas, nuts and lots of crumbs,
You stir it left, you stir it right,
You need to stay up half the night,
Taste the dish and make a wish
To keep your Christmas bright!

My mother bakes a pudding, it is tiny,
It's very small
 *Chorus* It's very small

My brother bakes a pudding, oh, cor blimey
It fills the hall
 *Chorus* It fills the hall

Granny takes her time and uses honey
It's very thick
 *Chorus* It's very thick

Sister's is like slime and very runny
It makes you sick
 *Chorus* It makes you sick

Tame it, flame it, with whisky made with malt,
Suet, cruet, don't forget the salt,
With milk and peel and eggs and spice
It's bound to taste most awfully nice,
Deck'd with holly, very jolly,
It's my Christmas vice.

Boil, it, broil it, cook it till it steams,
Coat it, float it on custards and on creams,
With lemon and lime and lots of time,
To make your recipe in rhyme,
Make it merry with a cherry,
Christmas pudding time. Oi!

*And for those far away ...*

## AN ANTARCTIC CHRISTMAS
*Dr Edward Wilson*

*Thursday 25 December 1902.* Christmas Day. Just gone midnight. A Merry Christmas to all at home. We are in our bags writing up diaries, looking forward to full meals for once. Turned out at 9 a.m. to a glorious Christmas of blazing sunshine. We were cooked by it all day, except while we were cooking. We had three hot meals! I read Holy Communion and various other things in my bag before we turned out.

Our meals must be given in detail as they were very exceptionally good today. I cooked the breakfast. We had tea, extra strong and sweet. (Milk of course we haven't had since we left the ship.) Biscuit, and a pannikin full of biscuit crumbs, bacon and seal liver fried up in pemmican. To top up we each had a spoonful of blackberry jam from a tin we brought specially for this day, our only tin.

After breakfast we grouped ourselves in front of the camp and let off the camera by a string, flying all our flags and the Union Jack. We then did a good 6 miles' march and camped for lunch in great heat. We had a brew of Bovril chocolate and plasmon [a protein supplement], biscuit and more blackberry jam. The Captain [Robert Falcon Scott] took a sight and I made a sketch, but my left eye is useless. We then did 4 miles and camped for the night at 8.30 p.m., having covered 10 miles in from 6 to 7 hours, a great improvement …

Shackle cooked our supper. We had three NAO rations, with biscuit and a tomato soup square from our 'Hoosh McGoo'. Then a very small plum pudding, the size of a cricket ball, with biscuit and the remains of the blackberry jam and two pannikins of cocoa with plasmon. We meant to have had some brandy alight on the plum pudding, but all our brandy has turned black in its tin for some reason, so we left it alone. We enjoyed our Christmas, though so far from home.

*And a final Christmas wish in the words of an old Gaelic blessing …*

> May the road rise up to meet you
> May the sun shine always on your face
> May the wind be always at your back
> May the rains fall gently on your field and
>     gardens:
> And until we meet again …
> … may God keep you
> in the hollow of His hand.

*Merry Christmas!*

# Acknowledgements

The publishers would like to thank the following for permission to reproduce copyright material. Every effort has been made to trace and contact copyright holders but in a few cases this has proved impossible. The publishers would like to hear from any copyright holders not here acknowledged.

22. 'Christmas' from *Collected Poems* by John Betjeman. Reproduced by permission of John Murray Publishers.

28. 'Snowflakes' from *An English Year* by Clive Sansom (Chatto). Reprinted by permission of David Higham Associates.

29. 'An Atrocious Institution', extract from 'Mrs Tanqueray Plays the Piano' by George Bernard Shaw. Reprinted by permission of the Society of Authors on behalf of the Bernard Shaw Estate.

30. 'Missiles Through the Post' by Cassandra from the *Daily Mirror*, 21 December 1953. Reprinted by permission of Mirrorpix.

31. 'The Boy Actor' from *Collected Verse* by Noël Coward (Methuen Publishing Ltd). Copyright © The Estate of Noël Coward.

34. 'Christmas in Wartime' by Mollie Panter-Downes, the London correspondent of the *New Yorker* magazine. Reprinted by permission of Lady Baer.

46. 'On Christmas Night …'. Collected by Ralph Vaughan Williams. Reproduced by courtesy of Stainer & Bell Ltd, London, England.

47. Extract from *Cider with Rosie* by Laurie Lee. Copyright © The Estate of Laurie Lee 1959. Reprinted by permission of PFD (www.pfd. co.uk) on behalf of The Estate of Laurie Lee.

57. 'A Christmas Carol' from *The Collected Poems of G.K. Chesterton*. Reprinted by permission of A.P. Watt on behalf of The Royal Literary Fund.

65. 'Wenceslas: the Inside Story' by Oliver Pritchett from the *Sunday Telegraph*, 21 December 1986. Reprinted by permission of the *Sunday Telegraph*.

90. 'All the Days of Christmas'. Copyright © Phyllis McGinley. First appeared in *Merry Christmas, Happy New Year*, published by Viking Press. Reprinted by permission of Curtis Brown, Ltd.

92. 'Albert and the Liner' from *Mondays, Thursdays* by Keith Waterhouse (Michael Joseph, 1976). Copyright © Keith Waterhouse 1976. Reprinted by permission of David Higham Associates.

105. 'Toys and Tangerines' from *A Child's Christmas in Wales* by Dylan Thomas (Orion). Copyright © 1954 by New Directions Publishing Corp. Reprinted by permission of New Directions Publishing Corp and David Higham Associates.

106. 'Christmas Thank Yous' by Mick Gowar. Reprinted by permission of the author.

122. 'What Do I Wish You?' by Charlotte Gray. Copyright © 1992. Used with permission of Helen Exley Giftbooks.

125. Extract from *The Growing Pains of Adrian Mole* by Sue Townsend. Reprinted by permission of The Random House Group Ltd.

129. Extract from *The Diary of a Provincial Lady* by E.M. Delafield. Copyright © The Estate of E.M. Delafield 1930. Reproduced by permission of Time Warner Books UK and PFD (www.pfd.co.uk) on behalf of The Estate of E.M. Delafield.

131. 'Christmas Day, 1955', extract from *The Noël Coward Diaries* © 1982 NC Aventales AG. Reprinted by kind permission of NC Aventales AG as Successor in Title to The Estate of Noël Coward and Sheridan Morley.

157. 'What the Donkey Saw' by U.A. Fanthorpe from *Christmas Poems* (2002). Copyright © U.A. Fanthorpe. Reproduced by permission of Peterloo Poets.

162. 'A Yorkshire Nativity' from *Head over Heels In the Dales* by Gervase Phinn. Reproduced by kind permission of the author.

165. 'The Barn' by Elizabeth Coatsworth from *Compass Rose*. Copyright © 1929 by Coward, McCann, Inc., © renewed 1957 by Elizabeth Coatsworth.

167. 'A Shepherd' from *Collected Edition of Heywood Broun* compiled by Heywood Hale Brown. Copyright © 1941 by Heywood Hale Broun.

170. 'Jesus' Christmas Party' from *Jesus' Christmas Party* by Nicholas Allan (Red Fox, 1996). Copyright © Nicholas Allan 1990. Reprinted by permission of A.M. Heath & Co. Ltd.

182. 'Christmas Day' by Roy Fuller. Reprinted by permission of John Fuller.

183. 'Remember Them' by Pam Brown. Copyright © 1992. Used with permission of Helen Exley Giftbooks.

.... and that,
I think,
is a
full
stocking !